Passing CTLLS Assessments

Passing CTLLS Assessments

Ann Gravells and Susan Simpson

LearningMatters

First published in 2011 by Learning Matters Ltd

British Library Cataloguing in Publication Data
A CIP record for this book is available from the British Library

ISBN: 978 0 85725 369 9

This book is available in the following ebook formats:

Adobe ebook ISBN: 9780857253712
EPUB ebook ISBN: 9780857253705
Kindle ISBN: 9780857253729

Cover and text design by Topics – the Creative Partnership
Project Management by Deer Park Productions
Typeset by Pantek Arts Ltd, Maidstone, Kent
Printed and bound in Great Britain by Bell & Bain Ltd, Glasgow

Learning Matters Ltd
20 Cathedral Yard
Exeter EX1 1HB
Tel: 01392 215560
info@learningmatters.co.uk
www.learningmatters.co.uk

Mixed Sources
Product group from well-managed
forests and other controlled sources
www.fsc.org Cert no. TT-COC-002769
© 1996 Forest Stewardship Council
FSC

CONTENTS

ACKNOWLEDGEMENTS

The authors would like to thank the following for their support and encouragement while writing this book.

Jennifer Clark
Angela Faulkener
Peter Frankish
Bob Gravells
Julia Morris
Amy Thornton
Jacklyn Williams
William Harrison
Rachel Simpson
Lindsay Simpson
Jennifer Davis
Lynne Maultby

The staff and learners of the teacher training department at Bishop Burton College and North East Lincolnshire Council's Community Learning Services.

Every effort has been made to trace the copyright holders and to obtain their permission for the use of copyright material. The publisher and author will gladly receive any information enabling them to rectify any error or omission in subsequent editions.

AUTHOR STATEMENTS

Ann Gravells is a lecturer in teacher training at Bishop Burton College in East Yorkshire. She has been teaching since 1983. She is a consultant to City & Guilds for various projects as well as externally verifying the City & Guilds teacher training qualifications. Ann holds a Masters in Educational Management, a PGCE, a Degree in Education, and a City & Guilds Medal of Excellence for teaching. Ann is a Fellow of the Institute for Learning and holds QTLS status.

She is the author of:

- *Preparing to Teach in the Lifelong Learning Sector;*
- *Principles and Practice of Assessment in the Lifelong Learning Sector;*
- *Delivering Employability Skills in the Lifelong Learning Sector;*
- *Passing PTLLS Assessments.*

She is co-author of:

- *Planning and Enabling Learning in the Lifelong Learning Sector;*
- *Equality and Diversity in the Lifelong Learning Sector.*

She has edited:

- *Study Skills for PTLLS.*

Ann welcomes any comments from readers; please contact her via her website: www.anngravells.co.uk.

Susan Simpson is a teacher in teacher training at the North East Lincolnshire Council's Community Learning Services in Grimsby. She has been teaching since 1980. Susan is currently Head of Community Learning Services and has been a Curriculum Manager for Education and Training, ICT, and Business Administration and Law for five years. She developed, managed and taught adult education programmes in Botswana for ten years. Susan has also presented at regional level for teacher training and nationally for ICT Skills for Life. Susan holds a Post Graduate Diploma in Management Studies, BA (Hons) in Further Education and Training, and Certificate in Education (Hons) in Business Studies and Economics.

She is co-author of:

- *Planning and Enabling Learning in the Lifelong Learning Sector;*
- *Equality and Diversity in the Lifelong Learning Sector.*

In this chapter you will learn about:

● the structure of the book and how to use it;

● preparing for your assessments;

● self-assessment activities and guidance for evidencing competence.

The structure of the book and how to use it

This book has been specifically written for associate teachers working towards the Certificate in Teaching in the Lifelong Learning Sector (CTLLS) qualification at either level 3 or 4. Prior to publication, it was announced by Lifelong Learning UK (LLUK) that the CTLLS units would be revised. Although the content of this book will still be applicable to the new units, the unit titles will change. The role of an Associate Teacher will not change, nor will the requirement to apply for your teaching status of Associate Teacher Learning and Skills (ATLS) through the Institute for Learning (IfL). LLUK ceased to exist after 31 March 2011.

Associate teachers do not perform as many roles as a full teacher, for example they might teach from pre-prepared materials whereas full teachers will create and use their own materials and resources. Full teachers must take the Diploma in Teaching in the Lifelong Learning Sector (DTLLS) qualification. If your role changes after completing the CTLLS qualification, you will need to take the DTLLS qualification (also known as the Certificate in Education or Post Graduate Certificate in Education). You will be able to carry forward two mandatory units and possibly one or two optional units that you have achieved as part of the CTLLS. Please see Chapter 13 for more details of the optional units. Whether you are part time or full time does not affect whether you are an associate or a full teacher. It is your job role that determines this.

Lifelong Learning UK (LLUK) identified the two teaching roles in the Further Education sector in England, for which there are government regulations.

● An associate teaching role has fewer teaching responsibilities and will be performed by those who are expected to gain the status of Associate Teacher, Learning and Skills (ATLS). An associate teacher will usually teach using materials prepared by others, on a one-to-one basis, or perhaps by delivering short programmes or assessing one subject.

- A full teaching role which represents the full range of responsibilities performed by those who are expected to gain the status of Qualified Teacher, Learning and Skills (QTLS). A full teacher will devise their own schemes of work, session plans, and teaching and learning materials. They will teach a variety of learners, subjects and levels, and contribute fully within the organisation through all stages of the teaching and learning cycle.

Once you have achieved your CTLLS qualification, you will need to undertake a probationary period before applying for your teaching status of ATLS through the Institute for Learning (IfL), you must also evidence the minimum core (see Chapter 13 for details).

The book is designed to help you assess the skills and knowledge you already have, in preparation for your formal CTLLS assessments. You must complete the mandatory unit of Preparing to Teach in the Lifelong Learning Sector (PTLLS) prior to, or as part of, the CTLLS qualification. A separate book *Passing PTLLS Assessments* (Gravells, 2010) is available to support the PTLLS Award.

This book will suit anyone taking the CTLLS qualification, whether as a short intensive programme of study, attending a formal programme over a number of weeks, or taking a distance, open or blended learning approach. The qualification can be delivered and assessed in a number of ways; however, the assessment criteria must be met whichever approach is taken.

Appendices 1, 2, 3 and 4 (pages 123–130) contain the CTLLS assessment criteria and self-audits at level 3 and level 4 for the two mandatory units of the CTLLS qualification: Planning and Enabling Learning in the Lifelong Learning Sector and Principles and Practice of Assessment in the Lifelong Learning Sector. Completing these self-audits will help you determine an appropriate level of achievement.

The book builds upon information in the companion textbooks *Preparing to Teach in the Lifelong Learning Sector* (Gravells, 2011a), *Planning and Enabling in the Lifelong Learning Sector* (Gravells and Simpson, 2010), and *Principles and Practice of Assessment in the Lifelong Learning Sector* (Gravells, 2011b). These books will help you understand the theory and practical requirements of teaching and assessing in the Lifelong Learning Sector.

Chapters 1–12 contain *self-assessment activities* based around the CTLLS assessment criteria. These are shown in boxes in each chapter for each level. You can then compare your responses with the *guidance for evidencing competence*. This will help you demonstrate and evidence your competence towards each learning outcome of the mandatory units. Additional guidance is given towards level 4 achievement and readers at this level can access and quote from the books and websites listed at the end of each chapter.

The book is not intended to give you the answers to questions you may be asked in any formal assessments; your responses will be specific to you, the subject you teach, and the context and environment in which you teach. The book will, however, guide you through the CTLLS learning outcomes with a view to helping you focus upon the requirements of the assessment criteria.

Chapter 13 contains useful information regarding the CTLLS qualification, such as details of the first mandatory unit of CTLLS: Preparing to Teach in the Lifelong Learning Sector (PTLLS), information regarding the optional units, teaching practice and observed practice. The minimum core of language, literacy, numeracy and information communication technology is also explored.

Appendices 5, 6, 7 and 8 (pages 131–146) contain examples of evidence which you could provide towards the assessment criteria at either level 3 or level 4.

Preparing for your assessments

Awarding Organisations take different approaches to assessment; however, the learning outcomes of the CTLLS qualification do not differ. Throughout your assessments, whether they are formal assignments, observations, questions, professional discussions with your assessor or another appropriate method, you will need to demonstrate you have met all the CTLLS assessment criteria at the level you wish to achieve.

If you would like to achieve CTLLS at level 4, you will need to be more analytical with your responses rather than just being descriptive. For example, level 3 assessment criteria might include the word *explain,* in which case it's fine to describe *what* you have done. At level 4, the assessment criteria might include the word *justify,* in which case you will need to describe *what* you have done and analyse *why* you did it that way. If you are aiming to achieve at level 4 you will need to carry out relevant research, reference your work to appropriate theorists, word-process your responses to questions and use an academic style of writing. The difference between the levels is expressed in the assessment criteria; the learning outcomes remain the same. The companion book *Study Skills for PTLLS* (Williams, 2010) should be of help.

As a starting point and to check the level you feel you could achieve, carry out an initial assessment by completing the self-audits in Appendices 1, 2, 3 and 4 (pages 123–130). These list the CTLLS learning outcomes and assessment criteria at both level 3 and level 4 respectively. By completing these, you will identify the level most suited to you for each unit. Read through each and note any evidence you currently have which meets the outcomes, along with the work you need to do to meet those left blank. Your evidence might be in the form of written responses or a reference to documents such as a session plan or observation report. It doesn't matter if you have lots of blank spaces at the moment; you are still learning and may not yet know how to achieve all the criteria. However, do remember if you wish to achieve at level 4 that your evidence must meet the level 4 requirements as stated in the previous paragraph.

Once you have worked through the self-assessment questions in Chapters 1–12, have another look at your self-audit and see if you can complete the blank spaces.

As you gain the skills and knowledge required, you will need to carry out various formal assessment activities, which will be issued to you at the training organisation you have enrolled with. These will differ depending upon which Awarding

Organisation you are registered with. They will usually consist of theory assessments which will test your knowledge of teaching and learning, and practical assessments which will test your ability to teach. You will need to check with your assessor if there is a wordcount for these and make sure you are within 10 per cent above or below it. You will also need to demonstrate and log at least 30 teaching practice hours, some of which will be observed by your assessor.

Self-assessment activities and guidance for evidencing competence

As you work through the self-assessment activities in each chapter, make sure your responses are specific to you and the subject you will teach. You should also refer to the context and environment in which you will teach. Examples of the context could be:

- Adult and Community Learning;
- Emergency, Public and Uniformed Services;
- Further Education College;
- Ministry of Defence/Armed Forces;
- Offender Learning;
- Sixth Form and Specialist Colleges;
- Training Organisation;
- Voluntary or Private Sector;
- Work-based Learning.

Examples of the environment include classrooms, community halls, outdoor spaces, training rooms, workshops and the work environment.

Once you have completed the self-assessment activities, check your responses with the guidance for evidencing competence. These are designed to help you focus upon the requirements of the assessment criteria. Your written responses should provide evidence of your knowledge; you will then need to provide evidence of your practice, for example your teaching materials and your assessor's observation reports.

Summary

In this chapter you have learnt about:

- the structure of the book and how to use it;
- preparing for your assessments;
- self-assessment activities and guidance for evidencing competence.

Theory focus

References and further information

Gravells A (2010) *Passing PTLLS Assessments.* Exeter: Learning Matters

Gravells A (2011a) *Preparing to Teach in the Lifelong Learning Sector* (4th edition). Exeter: Learning Matters

Gravells A (2011b) *Principles and Practice of Assessment in the Lifelong Learning Sector* (2nd edition). Exeter: Learning Matters

Gravells A and Simpson S (2010) *Planning and Enabling in the Lifelong Learning Sector* (2nd edition). Exeter: Learning Matters

Reece I and Walker S (2008) *Teaching, Training and Learning: a practical guide* (6th edition). Tyne and Wear: Business Education Publishers Ltd

Wallace S (2007) *Teaching, Tutoring and Training in the Lifelong Learning Sector* (3rd edition). Exeter: Learning Matters

Williams J (2010) *Study Skills for PTLLS.* Exeter: Learning Matters

Wilson, L (2008) *Practical teaching: a guide to PTLLS and CTLLS.* London: Cengage Learning

Websites

Awarding Organisations – www.ofqual.gov.uk/for-awarding-organisations

Institute for Learning – www.ifl.ac.uk

Lifelong Learning UK – www.lluk.org

The Further Education Teachers' Qualifications (England) Regulations 2007 – www.opsi.gov.uk/si/si2007/uksi_20072264_en_1

CHAPTER I
WAYS TO NEGOTIATE
APPROPRIATE INDIVIDUAL
GOALS WITH LEARNERS

This chapter is in two parts. The first part, **Self-assessment activities**, contains questions and activities which relate to the first learning outcome of the CTLLS mandatory unit: *Planning and Enabling Learning in the Lifelong Learning Sector – Understand ways to negotiate appropriate individual goals with learners*.

The assessment criteria for each level are shown in boxes and are followed by activities and questions for you to carry out. Ensure your responses are *specific to you*, the *subject* you will teach, and the *context* and *environment* in which you will teach.

After completing the activities and questions, check your responses with the second part: **Guidance for evidencing competence**. This guidance is not intended to give you the answers to questions you may be asked in any formal assessments; however, it will help you focus your responses towards meeting the CTLLS requirements.

Self-assessment activities

> Level 3 – 1.1 Explain the role of initial assessment in the learning and teaching process
>
> Level 4 – 1.1 Analyse the role of initial assessment in the learning and teaching process

Q1 Explain how the role of initial assessment is an important part of the learning and teaching process.

Q2 Analyse the benefits of initial assessment to the learning and teaching process.

Q3 What do you consider are the impacts of both good and bad initial assessment practice upon your learners?

> Level 3 – 1.2 Describe different methods of initial assessment for use with learners
>
> Level 4 –1.2 Describe and evaluate different methods of initial assessment for use with learners

Q4 Describe the different methods of initial and diagnostic assessments which are used in your organisation.

Q5 Demonstrate the use of different methods of initial assessment with your learners and evaluate how effective these were. Ensure your individual learning plans (ILP) and other documents show how initial assessment will be implemented and the results used.

> Level 3 – 1.3 Explain ways of planning, negotiating and recording appropriate learning goals with learners
>
> Level 4 – 1.3 Evaluate ways of planning, negotiating and recording appropriate learning goals with learners

Q6 Explain how you would move your learners on from initial assessment through the process of planning, negotiating and recording learning goals appropriate to their needs.

Q7 How would you ensure your learners are involved in making decisions about their learning?

Q8 What assessment tools could you use to ascertain whether appropriate learning goals had been agreed and were successful, i.e. how would you know that the methods you used worked for your learners?

Q9 Consider whether or not your organisation's ILP practice is already well developed or needs improving. If it needs improving, what would you suggest and why?

Guidance for evidencing competence

Level 3 – 1.1 Explain the role of initial assessment in the learning and teaching process

Level 4 – 1.1 Analyse the role of initial assessment in the learning and teaching process

Q1 Explain how the role of initial assessment is an important part of the learning and teaching process.

Your response should state that initial assessment is the first part of the teaching and learning cycle. It is carried out prior to or at the beginning of a programme to identify your learners' starting point, level and any particular requirements they may have. It is an important part of the learning and teaching process to ensure learners are enrolled on a programme which is suitable for them. Initial assessment of your learners' skills, knowledge and preferred learning styles should take place before you begin teaching the programme content. Some of your learners may not be very confident and may be returning to learning after a long break. However, if their first experience of assessment terrifies them, they may not return. It is very important to find out why they are interested in this programme and whether or not they have any prior knowledge or skills. Initial assessment is a process, not a single event. It should include assessment of literacy, language, numeracy and Information Communication Technology (ICT), along with a thorough diagnostic assessment of each learner's suitability for the programme or qualification they wish to achieve. It should also ascertain any particular learner needs or health concerns to enable appropriate support, for example a learner may need privacy to take insulin.

If a learner has evidence of prior knowledge or skills, this could be recognised to save any duplication of work. This process is known as *recognition of prior learning* (RPL).

At level 4, in addition to the above, you should read relevant textbooks, articles and journals, and access appropriate websites, referring to them in your response. When writing, you should be analytical rather than descriptive and use a recognised academic style of writing.

For example, you could analyse what theorists and organisations say about the impact of initial assessment on your learners. You could compare and contrast these and consider why some methods work better than others.

Q2 Analyse the benefits of initial assessment to the learning and teaching process.

The benefits of carrying out initial assessment include the opportunity to meet and begin a professional relationship with your learners. In your response, you need to analyse how initial assessment will ascertain and identify any learner needs by using a range of tests, questionnaires and interview techniques. This should ensure that, if there are any adjustments to be made, these can be organised and resolved before the first session. It is important for your learners to recognise that assessment starts prior to or at the beginning of the programme and is continuous throughout. By carrying out this process, you are showing your learners that their past experiences are valued and count towards their starting point. Each learner's goals and targets will then be progressively built upon throughout their time with you. Effective practice at the initial assessment stage will clarify each learner's needs, and also identify opportunities to support the development of other skills throughout the learning programme.

At level 4, in addition to the above, you should read relevant textbooks, articles and journals, and access appropriate websites, referring to them in your response. When writing, you should be analytical rather than descriptive and use a recognised academic style of writing.

For example, you could produce a case study regarding the types of initial assessments you used with your learners and analyse how the results benefitted the teaching and learning process.

Q3   What do you consider are the impacts of both good and bad initial assessment practice upon your learners?

If initial assessment is good it will convince your learners that they can confidently start the programme and work towards the necessary skills and knowledge to successfully achieve the required outcome. If they have any particular requirements, they should confidently know that they will be dealt with and any action necessary to address them will be taken. Your learners should be fully informed about what is expected of them and what they can expect from you and your organisation to support them towards successful achievement.

If initial assessment is bad, some of your learners might not return to your sessions, or they might take a programme or qualification which is not suitable for them. They might leave and become a withdrawal statistic and thus cause an impact upon your organisation's retention and achievement targets. If the initial assessment does not engage your learners in a non-threatening way and at an appropriate level, they may be disadvantaged. They may have been given an ILP in which inappropriate targets are set, which may result in your learners either not achieving them or struggling to do so.

At level 4, in addition to the above, you should read relevant textbooks, articles and journals, and access appropriate websites, referring to them in your response. When writing, you should be analytical rather than descriptive and use a recognised academic style of writing.

For example, you could research other types of initial assessment which have not been mentioned here and compare and contrast these with those used in your own organisation.

> Level 3 – 1.2 Describe different methods of initial assessment for use with learners
>
> Level 4 – 1.2 Describe and evaluate different methods of initial assessment for use with learners

Q4 Describe the different methods of initial and diagnostic assessments which are used in your organisation.

When responding to this question, you will benefit most by finding out what happens in a diverse range of subject specialist areas within your organisation. It is important to share in the good practice already being used by experienced teachers in your organisation. However, also think about whether there are more creative and interesting ways to engage your learners in this process. You could read your organisation's last Ofsted and/or Awarding Organisation's reports to find out what judgements they made regarding this process and what could be done to improve it. Some types of assessments can also identify learners with dyslexia, dyspraxia, dysgraphia, dyscalculia, etc. Knowing this will help you plan their learning journey effectively. You may need to communicate with more experienced staff who can give support as you will not be an expert in all areas.

Different initial and diagnostic methods include:

- aptitude tests;
- competence and skills tests;
- discussions, i.e. health concerns;
- evidence based for RPL;
- formal and informal assessments;
- interviews;
- online tests, i.e. learning styles;
- practical tests;
- profiling;
- screening, i.e. literacy, language, numeracy and ICT.

You could observe more experienced teachers carrying out some of the above. You might see things you had not considered doing or aspects you could improve on. You should find out what your organisation's policies and procedures are for initial and diagnostic assessments and state the differences between them. Ascertaining the learning styles of your learners will help ensure you are using appropriate methods for learning to take place. If you have a group of kinesthetic learners you would not be helping them by using theoretical teaching methods.

At level 4, in addition to the above, you should read relevant textbooks, articles and journals, and access appropriate websites, referring to them in your response. When writing, you should be analytical rather than descriptive and use a recognised academic style of writing.

For example, you could produce a case study evaluating how effective your organisation's initial assessment policies and procedures are, and make recommendations for improvement.

Q5 Demonstrate the use of different methods of initial assessment with your learners and evaluate how effective these were. Ensure your ILPs and other documents show how initial assessment will be implemented and the results used.

This is a practical task enabling you to demonstrate the use of different methods of initial assessment. You are required to deliver at least 30 teaching practice hours throughout your time working towards the CTLLS qualification. You will be observed by your assessor for some of this time and they will need to see that you have used different types and methods of assessment, including initial assessment. They will give you verbal and written feedback and you should take this into account when reflecting how effective the initial assessment was. You could write a self-evaluation or reflective learning journal to discuss how the initial assessment met the individual needs of your learners during a particular session. Evidence you could provide includes your scheme of work, session plans and ILPs showing how the initial assessment will be used, along with the actual initial assessment activities and an analysis of the results (do maintain confidentiality). You could also deliver a short micro-teach session to your peers to demonstrate your knowledge of different types of initial assessment.

At level 4, in addition to the above, you should read relevant textbooks, articles and journals, and access appropriate websites, referring to them in your response. When writing, you should be analytical rather than descriptive and use a recognised academic style of writing.

For example, you could keep an ongoing reflective learning journal throughout your time taking the CTLLS qualification and refer to how you use initial assessments and ILPs when writing these. You could also research how other educational establishments carry out initial assessments and compare and contrast these to your own.

> Level 3 – 1.3 Explain ways of planning, negotiating and recording appropriate learning goals with learners
>
> Level 4 – 1.3 Evaluate ways of planning, negotiating and recording appropriate learning goals with learners

Q6 Explain how you would move your learners on from initial assessment through the process of planning, negotiating and recording learning goals appropriate to their needs.

Your response should consider what your learners want to achieve and how this fits with the programme content and assessment criteria as determined by the Awarding Organisation. You need to know what you are going to teach, and your learners need to know what they are going to learn. The most effective way of moving your learners on is to set learning goals or targets, i.e. smaller steps of learning that your learners know they can achieve. These should be formally negotiated, agreed and celebrated once they have been achieved. A supportive and respectful relationship between your learners and yourself will ensure realistic goals and targets are agreed, along with how their progress will be assessed and recorded. You should discuss with your learners what they want to achieve in the short term and what they want to aspire to in the long term. Achievement of learning goals can then be planned which encompass the whole programme. You need to ensure your learners have every opportunity to contribute to the success of their learning, by actively involving them in making decisions throughout the programme.

Your programme may have an allocation of guided learning hours (GLH) or contact/non-contact hours, which is the number of hours within which your learners are expected to achieve the learning outcomes or qualification. The hours are sometimes dictated by the Qualifications and Credit Framework (QCF) and the amount of funding your organisation receives is usually based on these.

When agreeing targets, these should always be SMART (specific, measurable, achievable, realistic and time bound). This will ensure everyone is clear about what is going to be achieved and why, when, where and how.

At level 4, in addition to the above, you should read relevant textbooks, articles and journals, and access appropriate websites, referring to them in your response. When writing, you should be analytical rather than descriptive and use a recognised academic style of writing.

For example, you could evaluate the whole process of initial assessment, i.e. what effect the practice of planning, negotiating and recording learning goals has had upon your learners. You could produce a case study relating to particular learners from when they commenced to when they completed.

Q7 How would you ensure your learners are involved in making decisions about their learning?

Learners should be involved in making decisions about their learning to encourage them to take ownership of the process of planning their learning journey. This might start at the recruitment and interview stage to ensure learners are capable of achieving their chosen goals. Once accepted, you will need to negotiate and agree their goals and targets, and assess their progress continuously. During the early stages, it may take time to encourage your learners to actively participate in taking control of their learning; however, the benefits are exceptional if together you can work on this as a team. Convince your learners that they have choices and can direct their learning. Help them take ownership of their ILP so that it becomes theirs to record their agreed learning goals and the progress they are making towards achieving them. Outstanding practice happens where both you and your learners take an active role in this process. By the end of the programme the overall goals or targets should have been achieved, but with negotiation and direction from everyone involved along the way.

At level 4, in addition to the above, you should read relevant textbooks, articles and journals, and access appropriate websites, referring to them in your response. When writing, you should be analytical rather than descriptive and use a recognised academic style of writing.

For example, you could produce a case study regarding how you involved a particular learner (keeping their name confidential) in making decisions about their learning and how beneficial the process was to all concerned.

Q8   What assessment tools could you use to ascertain whether appropriate learning goals had been agreed and were successful, i.e. how would you know that the methods you used worked for your learners?

Assessment tools are the resources you use, for example to set and monitor targets. You would need to ascertain what targets have been set for your programmes and why. This could be due to external factors such as funding, or internal factors such as local employer demands. It is important that all targets are agreed and recorded whether they are hard targets, i.e. directly based on the curriculum, or soft targets, i.e. personal and social goals. If you are teaching a programme which does not lead to a formal qualification, you will still need to record learner targets and progress. This is known as *recognising and recording progress and achievement in non-accredited learning* (RARPA).

Adults will usually leave if their needs are not being met; therefore if anyone leaves, this may show that your learners were not on the right programme to start with. This will affect your retention rates. Achievement is another tool used to measure a programme's success – you need to ascertain if all your learners have achieved their planned learning goals, and if not, why not. You could state what needs to be improved for next time and why. Very often, organisations will withdraw poorly performing programmes because funding agencies only want to contract with organisations which have high success rates.

At level 4, in addition to the above, you should read relevant textbooks, articles and journals, and access appropriate websites, referring to them in your response. When writing, you should be analytical rather than descriptive and use a recognised academic style of writing.

For example, you could obtain, read and refer to internal reports from your organisation which relate to initial assessment, and analyse recruitment, retention and achievement statistics. Analysing these should help you appreciate why interviews and initial assessments are so crucial to a positive learning journey.

Q9 Consider whether or not your organisation's ILP practice is already well developed or needs improving. If it needs improving, what would you suggest and why?

Your response should consider current practice at your organisation regarding ILPs. All learners should have an ILP or an action plan, no matter which qualification or programme they are working towards. You should state what the current practice is, what is good about it and what could be improved and why. For example, you might feel some questions which are asked are no longer relevant, or a form needs changing to reflect the use of new technology.

All relevant information should be recorded on an ILP. The following is good practice.

- Involve your learners, encourage them to discuss their learning and support needs and to use their knowledge of their strengths and areas for development to set their own relevant learning targets.

- Refer to the results of initial and diagnostic assessments, along with learning styles tests to influence how they achieve their learning goals.

- Make sure they are individual to each learner; there is no one size fits all.

- Express and communicate learning targets both verbally and in writing to enable your learners to fully understand the requirements.

- Embed literacy, language, numeracy and ICT goals that are specific, clearly identified and relevant to your learners' needs and the demands of their programme goals.

- Ensure there is a clear link between the learning targets on the ILP, the teaching and learning process, and the qualification aims.

- Use regular tutorial and review sessions to update/amend the ILP with your learners.

- Ensure your learner has a copy of their ILP that they can refer to regularly.

At level 4, in addition to the above, you should read relevant textbooks, articles and journals, and access appropriate websites, referring to them in your response. When writing, you should be analytical rather than descriptive and use a recognised academic style of writing.

For example, you could ask your organisation's quality assurance team for access to a variety of anonymised ILPs and use the good practice bullet points (on the previous page) to evaluate them. You may be able to identify some gaps or suggest a more efficient way of updating and implementing them.

Theory focus

References and further information

Daines J, Daines C and Graham B (2006) *Adult Learning Adult Teaching* (4th edition). Cardiff: Welsh Academic Press

DfES (2004) *Planning Learning, Recording Progress and Reporting Achievement – a guide for practitioners*. London: DfES

Gravells A (2011) *Principles and Practice of Assessment in the Lifelong Learning Sector* (2nd edition). Exeter: Learning Matters

Gravells A and Simpson S (2010) *Planning and Enabling Learning in the Lifelong Learning Sector* (2nd edition). Exeter: Learning Matters

Knowles M, Holton E and Swanson R (2011) *The adult learner: the definitive classic in adult education and human resource development* (6th edition). Oxford: Butterworth-Heinemann

Mager R (1991) *Preparing instructional objectives* (2nd edition). London: Kogan Page

Minton D (2005) *Teaching Skills in Further and Adult Education* (3rd edition). Andover: Thomson Learning

Petty G (2009) *Teaching Today: A Practical Guide* (4th edition). Cheltenham: Nelson Thornes

Wallace S (2007) *Teaching, Tutoring and Training in the Lifelong Learning Sector* (3rd edition). Exeter: Learning Matters

Websites

Initial Assessment – www.excellencegateway.org.uk/page.aspx?o=barnsleymbcrarpa and http://golddust.bdplearning.com/assessment_for_learning/initial_assessment.php

Initial Assessment Tools – www.toolslibrary.co.uk

Learning Styles – www.vark-learn.com

Literacy and Numeracy online tests – www.move-on.org.uk

Qualifications and Credit Framework – www.qcda.gov.uk/qualifications/60.aspx

RARPA toolkit – www.ladder4learning.org.uk/resources/learning/rarpa

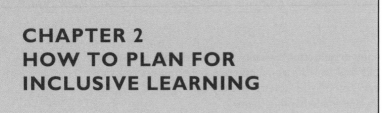

CHAPTER 2
HOW TO PLAN FOR
INCLUSIVE LEARNING

This chapter is in two parts. The first part, *Self-assessment activities*, contains questions and activities which relate to the second learning outcome of the CTLLS mandatory unit: *Planning and Enabling Learning in the Lifelong Learning Sector – Understand how to plan for inclusive learning*.

The assessment criteria for each level are shown in boxes and are followed by activities and questions for you to carry out. Ensure your responses are *specific to you*, the *subject* you will teach, and the *context* and *environment* in which you will teach.

After completing the activities and questions, check your responses with the second part: *Guidance for evidencing competence*. This guidance is not intended to give you the answers to questions you may be asked in any formal assessments; however, it will help you focus your responses towards meeting the CTLLS requirements.

Self-assessment activities

> Level 3 – 2.1 Establish and maintain an inclusive learning environment
>
> Level 4 – 2.1 Establish and maintain an inclusive learning environment

Q10 What does an inclusive learning environment mean for your learners and how does this impact on their learning?

Q11 Consider each stage of the teaching and learning cycle. Explore at each stage how you establish and maintain an inclusive learning environment.

Q12 In what ways can you make a difference which will ensure that all your learners feel they are in a learning environment which supports them to learn and achieve?

> Level 3 – 2.2 Devise a scheme of work which meets learners' needs and curriculum requirements
>
> Level 4 – 2.2 Devise and justify a scheme of work which meets learners' needs and curriculum requirements

Q13 What information would you need to be able to devise a scheme of work which will meet your learners' needs and your organisation's curriculum requirements?

Q14 Devise a scheme of work for your specialist subject to meet your learners' needs and your organisation's curriculum requirements. Justify why your scheme of work is fit for purpose.

> Level 3 – 2.3 Devise session plans which meet the aims and needs of learners
>
> Level 4 – 2.3 Devise and justify session plans which meet the aims and needs of individual learners and/or groups

Q15 Using your scheme of work, devise session plans for the first four weeks of the programme you are teaching.

Q16 Justify the factors you have taken into consideration when devising your session plans to ensure that they meet the aims and needs of individual learners and/or groups.

> Level 3 – 2.4 Explain ways in which session plans can be adapted to the individual needs of learners
>
> Level 4 – 2.4 Analyse ways in which session plans can be adapted to the individual needs of learners

Q17 There may be a need to adapt a session plan to meet the specific needs of individual learners. Explain how you would do this within your own specialist subject.

Q18 Analyse other ways in which adaptations can be made to meet the individual needs of learners.

> Level 3 – 2.5 Plan the use of a variety of delivery methods, explaining the choice
>
> Level 4 – 2.5 Plan the appropriate use of a variety of delivery methods, justifying the choice

Q19 How will you plan which delivery methods are most appropriate and effective for your specialist subject?

Q20 Justify why you have chosen these methods.

> Level 3 – 2.6 Identify opportunities for learners to provide feedback to inform practice
>
> Level 4 – 2.6 Identify and evaluate opportunities for learners to provide feedback to inform practice

Q21 What opportunities can you identify for your learners to provide feedback? Evaluate how these opportunities can inform practice.

Guidance for evidencing competence

Level 3 – 2.1 Establish and maintain an inclusive learning environment

Level 4 – 2.1 Establish and maintain an inclusive learning environment

Q10 What does an inclusive learning environment mean for your learners and how does this impact on their learning?

Your response should state that an inclusive learning environment means that all learners have had equal access to learning opportunities. You should have established that they are on the right programme and all reasonable adjustments have been made, preferably prior to their commencement. In your response you should consider how you and your learners are going to establish this. It might mean something different to each learner, for example for one learner it might mean signposting and referral to a more appropriate programme (or perhaps a different level). For another learner it might mean supporting them due to a physical disability. Inclusive learning is about recognising that each of your learners is different, and they should not be excluded from access to any activities within your sessions for any legitimate reason. Thorough and considered planning will ensure that as many barriers to learning as possible are either removed or minimised so that your learners can concentrate on their learning. It will also mean that your learners are more likely to regularly attend your programme and work towards a successful achievement. Adult learners have other important people and events in their lives that may impact on their ability to learn. Empathy, understanding and honesty from you will help your learners want to find solutions to enable them to continue with their learning.

At level 4, in addition to the above, you should read relevant textbooks, articles and journals, and access appropriate websites, referring to them in your response. When writing, you should be analytical rather than descriptive and use a recognised academic style of writing.

For example, you could refer to Maslow's Hierarchy of Needs discussed in his book *Motivation and Personality* (1954) to help you understand that not all of your learners will be at the same point in their lives. You can then analyse what impact this theory may have on your learners and their learning environment.

Q11 Consider each stage of the teaching and learning cycle. Explore at each stage how you establish and maintain an inclusive learning environment.

Your response should relate to the following stages.

Identifying needs

It is essential that your learners have had the benefit of appropriate careers and skills advice to fit their individual needs and enable them to embark on a programme of learning which is right for them. Appropriate initial assessment activities will aid this process, for example carrying out an initial interview, a literacy, numeracy and ICT skills assessment, a learning styles questionnaire or a written personal statement.

Planning learning

You should plan an effective scheme of work, session plans, activities and resources based upon your organisation's curriculum requirements and the needs of your learners. Your planning will be greatly influenced by the results from a variety of initial assessment activities. These should reflect inclusivity by ensuring that there is:

- something in your plan for all your learners, whatever their level of ability;

- variety in teaching and learning methods;

- activities and resources to suit all levels of ability;

- variety in the way in which your learners are assessed;

- reasonable adjustments to the learning environment to ensure it is accessible;

- adequate additional learning support for those learners who may need it;

- an opportunity for your learners to give feedback on your programme.

Enabling learning

Enabling is about the actual teaching and learning taking place. To ensure you are being inclusive during this stage you should create, design and/or select appropriate resources and activities which will reflect the social and cultural aspects of the group. For example, you may have learners from a variety of cultural backgrounds and be able to use this to enhance learning activities and resources. It may be necessary to organise specialist help for learners who may require additional learning support. Your planning needs to be varied and engage with the principles of active learning.

Assessing learning

The types of assessment will vary depending upon the subject you are teaching and assessing. The most commonly used ones are initial (at the beginning), formative (ongoing) and summative (at the end). You will need to state which assessment types you plan to use and how they can effectively meet the needs of your individual learners. You need to plan the methods you will use, for example observation, assignments, tests. When planning assessment, you need to make sure the types and methods are valid and reliable, and that you are being fair and ethical with all your decisions to ensure you are being inclusive and differentiating for any learner needs.

- Valid – the assessment type and method is appropriate to the subject/qualification being assessed.

- Reliable – if the assessment is carried out again with similar learners, similar results will be achieved.

- Fair – the assessment type and method is appropriate to all your learners at the required level, is inclusive, i.e. available to all, and differentiates for any particular needs.

- Ethical – the assessment takes into account confidentiality, integrity, safety and security.

Quality assurance and evaluation

There will be processes of quality assurance in your organisation which may involve observations of your teaching and learning by your mentor, a manager or more experienced colleagues. There should be opportunities for comments and suggestions from your learners about their experiences on your programme, for example through questionnaires. These processes, along with your own reflections, self-assessment and organisational practices, will contribute to improvements in the quality of the learning programme and experiences for the learner.

At level 4, in addition to the above, you should read relevant textbooks, articles and journals, and access appropriate websites, referring to them in your response. When writing, you should be analytical rather than descriptive and use a recognised academic style of writing.

For example, you could research the impact of the theories of active learning on the motivation of your learners. Geoff Petty, on his website states that *what the learner does is more important than what the teacher does* (geoffpetty.com). In your response you could analyse how you can implement active learning in your specialist subject area.

Q12 In what ways can you make a difference which will ensure that all your learners feel they are in a learning environment which supports them to learn and achieve?

Your response should show that it is your responsibility to ensure that you provide an inclusive learning environment and equality of opportunity in all aspects of the learning experience. The way in which you can make a difference is to ensure that the learning environment evolves from and around the learner. You need to devise your programme of activity around the teaching and learning cycle, i.e. how you plan a structured programme around the *learner* not around the *teacher* or the *programme*. You should create a learning environment in which independence is cultivated and grows so that your learners know that they can go out into the world with the skills and knowledge they have learnt and be able to use them.

At level 4, in addition to the above, you should read relevant textbooks, articles and journals, and access appropriate websites, referring to them in your response. When writing, you should be analytical rather than descriptive and use a recognised academic style of writing.

For example, you could refer to and discuss the Personalised Learning Agenda for Adults at the shortcut http://tiny.cc/zhqbb. This supports the delivery of quality learning programmes that are personalised and appropriate to each learner's needs and which support social inclusion and social mobility. You could reflect on these concepts and discuss with colleagues the challenges of how this fits in with the teaching and learning cycle.

Level 3 – 2.2 Devise a scheme of work which meets learners' needs and curriculum requirements

Level 4 – 2.2 Devise and justify a scheme of work which meets learners' needs and curriculum requirements

---

Q13 What information would you need to be able to devise a scheme of work which will meet your learners' needs and your organisation's curriculum requirements?

Your response should state that you would:

- obtain the most recent handbook from the Awarding Organisation, which contains details and guidance on procedures, the syllabus and the assessment requirements and strategy;

- find out if there are professional bodies responsible for identifying and monitoring the standards in your subject area;

- find out what internal quality assurance procedures are in place at your organisation for monitoring your programme;

- plan the dates and times of delivery for each of your sessions, taking into account bank/public/religious holidays, assessment target dates, etc.;

- find out what environment/rooms, resources, equipment, etc. are available, along with any health and safety requirements, and facilities that your learners can access;

- find out if there is a dedicated curriculum team of experienced colleagues or staff who can support and help both you and your learners.

You may be teaching a programme without a recognised qualification; however, you will still be required to find out if there is an existing syllabus or if you need to design your own. In the case of the latter, there will probably be organisational requirements for you to follow to ensure you teach your subject correctly.

You need to find out what information your organisation collects about your learners before they arrive at the first session, for example initial assessment, and use this to help you plan to meet their requirements.

You may be employed as an associate teacher and be required to work from pre-prepared schemes of work and session plans. However, it is a useful skill to be able to plan your own sessions and take control of the content. You may need to make necessary adjustments depending on the needs of your learners – every learner and every group is different.

At level 4, in addition to the above, you should read relevant textbooks, articles and journals, and access appropriate websites, referring to them in your response. When writing, you should be analytical rather than descriptive and use a recognised academic style of writing.

For example, you could research the website of your specialist subject Sector Skills Council and find out if there is any sharing of good practice through case studies and materials. Evaluate the relevance of these materials in relation to your scheme of work. You could also review schemes of work produced by colleagues for your subject area to ensure you are standardising practice.

Q14 Devise a scheme of work for your specialist subject to meet your learners' needs and your organisation's curriculum requirements. Justify why your scheme of work is fit for purpose.

This is a practical task to create a scheme of work which you will be able to put forward as evidence providing it meets the requirements of the CTLLS qualification. Your scheme of work should be based upon your specialist subject and meet the requirements of the Awarding Organisation and/or your organisation's curriculum requirements.

Your response should consider and justify factors from the perspective of the learner and your organisation's curriculum. For example, matching the number of hours the programme is funded for (if applicable), how many hours each learner will need (based on their initial assessment) and to fulfil the Awarding Organisation's syllabus requirements (if you are teaching an accredited qualification).

At level 4, in addition to the above, you should read relevant textbooks, articles and journals, and access appropriate websites, referring to them in your response. When writing, you should be analytical rather than descriptive and use a recognised academic style of writing.

For example, you could analyse the key principles of adult learning, based on the work of the American writer Malcolm Knowles (1913–97), and how they might affect the way you produce a scheme of work. The key principles for successful adult learning are linked to what adults themselves say about their learning.

Level 3 – 2.3 Devise session plans which meet the aims and needs of learners

Level 4 – 2.3 Devise and justify session plans which meet the aims and needs of individual learners and/or groups

Q15 Using your scheme of work, devise session plans for the first four weeks of the programme you are teaching.

This is a practical task to create session plans which you will be able to put forward as evidence providing they meet the requirements of the CTLLS qualification.

Your session plans will contain more detail than your scheme of work for a particular teaching session, but the two documents should relate to each other. You may be required to work from pre-prepared session plans. However, it is a useful skill to be able to plan your own sessions and take control of the content. You may need to make necessary adjustments depending on the needs of your learners – every learner and every group is different.

It is crucial to prepare your session plans well, to enable effective teaching and learning to take place.

At level 4, in addition to the above, you should read relevant textbooks, articles and journals, and access appropriate websites, referring to them in your response. When writing, you should be analytical rather than descriptive and use a recognised academic style of writing.

For example, you could refer to and discuss case studies in relevant textbooks or journals which explore various types of planning documents and those which are most relevant and effective for your learners in your specialist area.

Q16 Justify the factors you have taken into consideration when devising your session plans to ensure that they meet the aims and needs of individual learners and/or groups.

Your response should justify why your session plan should be fit for purpose in such a way that the learning taking place is set in a realistic context for the programme and/or qualification, while meeting the individual needs of your learners. Your learners will have divulged information during induction and initial assessment which will assist you in your planning, for example their previous learning experiences and any concerns about their literacy, language, numeracy or ICT skills. During the first session you could encourage your learners to share information about their interests and hobbies and what their aspirations are, perhaps as part of an icebreaker activity. This will help you get to know your learners, enabling you to individualise learning as necessary. Effective teaching and learning is a result of careful planning and preparation, and it is your responsibility to ensure that this is completed in plenty of time before teaching your session.

You should have considered the following factors:

- preferred learning styles, initial assessment and prior knowledge and skills;
- any support required;

- using practical activities that link to real work experiences, if appropriate;

- equality and diversity, for example how you could take into account any naturally occurring opportunities such as current news stories or particular events;

- functional skills, how you can embed English, maths and ICT within your sessions;

- inviting guest speakers, for example past learners who have progressed further, or local employers who can explain job prospects;

- differentiating activities, tasks, resources, assessments, etc. for individuals and groups;

- the beginning, middle and end to your session – these should be structured and logical.

At level 4, in addition to the above, you should read relevant textbooks, articles and journals, and access appropriate websites, referring to them in your response. When writing, you should be analytical rather than descriptive and use a recognised academic style of writing.

For example, you could produce a case study or discuss in your reflective learning journal how you devised your session plans to meet the aims and needs of individual learners and/or groups for your particular subject.

Level 3 – 2.4 Explain ways in which session plans can be adapted to the individual needs of learners

Level 4 – 2.4 Analyse ways in which session plans can be adapted to the individual needs of learners

---

Q17 There may be a need to adapt a session plan to meet the specific needs of individual learners. Explain how you would do this within your own specialist subject.

Your response should explain how you would adapt an aspect of a particular session plan as a result of becoming aware of a specific need of a learner or learners. For example, you might ascertain from assessing your learners' written work that many of them are having difficulty with spelling and grammar, and therefore have not successfully met the assessment criteria. You could adapt the next session plan to incorporate revision and further assessment before moving your learners on. You might then decide that you will need support from a specialist and use your organisation's referral procedures to arrange appropriate support.

At level 4, in addition to the above, you should read relevant textbooks, articles and journals, and access appropriate websites, referring to them in your response. When writing, you should be analytical rather than descriptive and use a recognised academic style of writing.

For example, you could refer to and discuss case studies in relevant textbooks or journals which particularly evaluate the benefits of collaborative teaching and learning in vocational specialist areas. You could explore how you think this might work with your own learners and consider how relevant it is.

Q18 Analyse other ways in which adaptations can be made to meet the individual needs of learners.

Your response should analyse what has been achieved, what went particularly well and what did not go well for all of your learners in each of your sessions. You should explain how you will make changes if you deliver this same session again and what you will do to implement them, for example changing the font size in handouts, reducing the amount of jargon used, amending the level of an activity, incorporating technology and adapting equipment to make it accessible to everyone. You might need to liaise with others to make adaptations.

You could give examples of whether or not you need to address any gaps in your own skills and knowledge and how you will engage with this in your continuing professional development (CPD).

At level 4, in addition to the above, you should read relevant textbooks, articles and journals, and access appropriate websites, referring to them in your response. When writing, you should be analytical rather than descriptive and use a recognised academic style of writing.

For example, you could refer to and discuss case studies in relevant textbooks or journals which consider learners who have learning difficulties and/or disabilities. You could state what adaptations, if any, you would need to make to your planning to ensure that the learning environment is fully inclusive in these circumstances. You could also cite relevant legislation such as the Disability Discrimination Act (2005) and Equality and Diversity Act (2010).

Level 3 – 2.5 Plan the use of a variety of delivery methods, explaining the choice

Level 4 – 2.5 Plan the appropriate use of a variety of delivery methods, justifying the choice

---

Q19 How will you plan which delivery methods are most appropriate and effective for your specialist subject?

The teaching and learning activities you use should be matched against your learners preferred learning styles and be relevant for the subject they are taking. You should use varied activities to reach all learning styles such as discussions in groups, practical tasks, visual stimulus, theory, etc. When planning these activities, consider the three domains of learning, i.e. cognitive, affective and psychomotor (Bloom, 1956) and check that your session plans include a balance of these where appropriate. You also need to consider which delivery methods will be most effective in relation to your specialist subject. The learning environment and resources available may also have an impact on which delivery methods you select, for example if there is no internet connection available then you will not be able to plan to use web-based research as a teaching and learning activity.

At level 4, in addition to the above, you should read relevant textbooks, articles and journals, and access appropriate websites, referring to them in your response. When writing, you should be analytical rather than descriptive and use a recognised academic style of writing.

For example, you could explore Bloom's (1956) Taxonomy theory and the impact it might have upon why you chose particular delivery methods.

Q20 Justify why you have chosen these methods.

Your response should justify why you have chosen the teaching and learning activities mentioned in question 19. When you are deciding which methods will be most effective, consider your learners' needs and the needs of your organisation and the curriculum. Your session plans should provide a framework within which your learners can achieve their learning goals which, for most of them, will ultimately be the qualification. It is crucial that the methods are varied within sessions and the programme overall to provide challenges and stretch your learners. You may decide to try a new method on the basis that you are challenging your learners to engage in a new learning activity. An example of this would be role playing case studies rather than just discussing them. Justification for trying new activities will depend on the point at which you build this into your planning and how well you all know and trust each other.

At level 4, in addition to the above, you should read relevant textbooks, articles and journals, and access appropriate websites, referring to them in your response. When writing, you should be analytical rather than descriptive and use a recognised academic style of writing.

For example, you could research Tuckman's (1965) stages of group development and analyse what impact these different stages could have upon your learners. This clearly is a factor in your plans which would need constant review as groups develop in different ways and at a different pace. You may plan some teaching and learning activities which will need to be adapted because the group is not yet at the stage where the learners could effectively engage in a particular process.

> Level 3 – 2.6 Identify opportunities for learners to provide feedback to inform practice
>
> Level 4 – 2.6 Identify and evaluate opportunities for learners to provide feedback to inform practice

Q21 What opportunities can you identify for your learners to provide feedback? Evaluate how these opportunities can inform practice.

Your response should identify examples such as: appeals, comment cards, complaints, discussions, forums, notes, questionnaires, tutorial reviews and surveys. All these methods can be manual or electronic, formal or informal, to an individual or a group and anonymous or otherwise. You should identify what is used at your organisation at the moment, and what other opportunities there could be. You could consider innovative or different methods such as giving out sticky notes or comment cards for learners to write on as your session progresses or ends. They could state what they enjoy or what could be improved, and can remain anonymous to encourage honesty and openness. This method also encourages learners to write something down who might not feel confident talking to you or in front of their peers.

For each example you have listed, you should evaluate how the feedback can inform your practice. For example, encouraging your learners to talk to you after a session will gain immediate feedback enabling you to make any necessary changes before the next session. This should prevent an issue arising which might evolve into an appeal or a complaint.

At level 4, in addition to the above, you should read relevant textbooks, articles and journals, and access appropriate websites, referring to them in your response. When writing, you should be analytical rather than descriptive and use a recognised academic style of writing.

For example, you could research different methods of designing surveys and questionnaires, create and implement one with your learners, analyse the results and produce a summary report and action plan.

Theory focus

References and further information

Bloom B (ed) (1956) *Taxonomy of Educational Objectives, the classification of educational goals – Handbook I: Cognitive Domain.* New York: McKay

Daines J, Daines C and Graham B (2006) *Adult Learning Adult Teaching* (4th edition). Cardiff: Welsh Academic Press

Duckett I and Jones C (2006) *Personalised learning: meeting individual learner needs.* London: Learning and Skills Network

Gravells A (2011) *Preparing to Teach in the Lifelong Learning Sector* (4th edition). Exeter: Learning Matters

Knowles M (1996) *The adult learner: a neglected species* (4th edition). Houston: Gulf Publishing

Maslow A (1954) *Motivation and Personality* (3rd edition). Hong Kong: Longman

Minton D (2005) *Teaching Skills in Further and Adult Education* (3rd edition). Andover: Thomson Learning

Tomlinson M (2006) *Inclusive Learning.* Further Education Funding Council, Learning Difficulties and/or Disabilities Committee

Tuckman B (1965) Developmental sequence in small groups. *Psychological bulletin,* 63: 384–99

Websites

Bloom's Taxonomy – www.businessballs.com/bloomstaxonomyoflearningdomains.htm

Disability Discrimination Act – http://www.opsi.gov.uk/Acts/acts2005/ukpga_20050013_en_1

Equality Act – www.equalities.gov.uk/equality_act_2010.aspx

Equality and Human Rights Commission – http://www.uk250.co.uk/frame/4060/disability-rights-commission.html

Foundation Learning Curriculum for adults – tiny.cc/zhqbb or readingroom.skillsfundingagency.bis.gov.uk/sfa/adult_flc_-_factsheet_-_april_10_-_final.doc

Geoff Petty – www.geoffpetty.com

Gold dust Resources for teacher educators – golddust.bdplearning.com/

Tuckman's group theories – www.infed.org/thinkers/tuckman.htm

CHAPTER 3
HOW TO USE TEACHING AND LEARNING STRATEGIES AND RESOURCES INCLUSIVELY TO MEET CURRICULUM REQUIREMENTS

This chapter is in two parts. The first part, **Self-assessment activities**, contains questions and activities which relate to the third learning outcome of the CTLLS mandatory unit: *Planning and Enabling Learning in the Lifelong Learning Sector – Understand how to use teaching and learning strategies and resources inclusively to meet curriculum requirements.*

The assessment criteria for each level are shown in boxes and are followed by activities and questions for you to carry out. Ensure your responses are *specific to you*, the *subject* you will teach and the *context* and *environment* in which you will teach.

After completing the activities and questions, check your responses with the second part: **Guidance for evidencing competence**. This guidance is not intended to give you the answers to questions you may be asked in any formal assessments; however, it will help you focus your responses towards meeting the CTLLS requirements.

Self-assessment activities

Level 3 – 3.1 Use a range of inclusive learning activities to enthuse and motivate learners, ensuring that curriculum requirements are met

Level 4 – 3.1 Select/adapt, use and justify a range of inclusive learning activities to enthuse and motivate learners, ensuring that curriculum requirements are met

Q22 During your teaching, demonstrate the use of a range of inclusive learning activities which meet the requirements of the curriculum. How will these enthuse and motivate your learners?

Q23 Justify the reasons why you selected, adapted and used the range of learning activities in question 22.

Level 3 – 3.2 Identify the strengths and limitations of a range of resources, including new and emerging technologies, showing how these resources can be used to promote equality, support diversity and contribute to effective learning

Level 4 – 3.2 Analyse the strengths and limitations of a range of resources, including new and emerging technologies, showing how these resources can be used to promote equality, support diversity and contribute to effective learning

Q24 Using a table similar to that below, identify a range of resources and state their strengths and limitations (include new and emerging technologies).

Resource	Strengths	Limitations

Q25 From the strengths and limitations identified in your table, analyse the overall contribution of each resource in terms of how they promote equality, support diversity and contribute to effective learning.

Level 3 – 3.3 Identify literacy, language, numeracy and ICT skills which are integral to own specialist area

Level 4 – 3.3 Identify literacy, language, numeracy and ICT skills which are integral to own specialist area, reviewing how they support learner achievement

Q26 Why is it important to assess the literacy, language, numeracy and ICT skills of your learners and how will embedding these in your programme support their achievement?

Q27 Using your current scheme of work and session plans, identify the opportunities for embedding and promoting literacy, language, numeracy and ICT skills and knowledge for your learners.

Level 3 – 3.4 Select/adapt and use a range of inclusive resources to promote inclusive learning and teaching

Level 4 – 3.4 Select/adapt, use and justify a range of inclusive resources to promote inclusive learning and teaching

Q28 Justify your reasons for selecting, adapting and using your resources to promote inclusive learning and teaching.

Guidance for evidencing competence

Level 3 – 3.1 Use a range of inclusive learning activities to enthuse and motivate learners, ensuring that curriculum requirements are met

Level 4 – 3.1 Select/adapt, use and justify a range of inclusive learning activities to enthuse and motivate learners, ensuring that curriculum requirements are met

Q22 During your teaching, demonstrate the use of a range of inclusive learning activities which meet the requirements of the curriculum. How will these enthuse and motivate your learners?

This is a practical task enabling you to use a range of activities which should enthuse and motivate your learners. Your evidence should demonstrate that you have used a range of learning activities that will include all your learners and are appropriate to the learning outcomes and assessment criteria identified in the curriculum. For example, if the learning outcome is *to build a wall* then your range of learning activities might include:

- demonstration;
- discussion;
- drawing;
- group work;
- handouts;
- instruction;
- journal or diary;
- practical tasks;
- projects;
- questions;
- quizzes;
- technology-based learning (using the internet and a DVD);
- tutorials;
- visiting speaker;
- visits or field trips;
- worksheets;
- workshops.

You should demonstrate how you stimulate and motivate your learners by using a variety of appropriate methods, which might include a blended learning approach of traditional and technology-based learning. You should also ensure you are challenging your learners to embrace new ideas and new ways of learning, while being inclusive and differentiating activities to meet all learners' requirements.

At level 4, in addition to the above, you should read relevant textbooks, articles and journals, and access appropriate websites, referring to them in your response. When writing, you should be analytical rather than descriptive and use a recognised academic style of writing.

For example, you could carry out a search via the internet for *theories of learning, personalised learning theories* and *motivation theorists*. You can then analyse how you can extend the range of learning activities you offer to your learners and what difference this will make to the way in which they participate in your sessions. You could also research different statements regarding inclusion. For example, *Inclusion simply means 'available to all'* (Wilson, 2008, p296), and *Inclusion involves finding ways to integrate learners with particular needs into mainstream provision* (Hill, 2010, p38). You could then compare and contrast your findings.

Q23 Justify the reasons why you selected, adapted and used the range of learning activities in question 22.

Your response should justify your reasons why, for example to differentiate the methods used to ensure they are appropriate to the subject and topic, and level and abilities of your learners. You could give examples of the activities you have used for your subject, stating how they included all your learners and enabled learning to take place. Using different teaching methods, combined with learner activities, will help reach the different learning styles of your individual learners. Your methods should always promote active learning. It is also important that the learning activities you select and use meet the requirements of the curriculum and the Awarding Organisation.

Laird (2003) suggests learning occurs when the senses of *sight, hearing, touch, smell* and *taste* are stimulated. You could try something different to make your sessions really interesting to motivate your learners. Whenever possible, link theory to practice, and use practical activities based around the subject and areas of interest of your learners. If you can make your sessions fun and interesting, relating to all the senses, it will help your learners remember the topics better. Do not forget two other senses you can use as a teacher: a sense of humour and common sense.

Experimenting with new or different teaching methods and activities will make your sessions interesting and should generate a vibrant environment and enthusiasm for learning. What really matters is what is being learnt. When choosing appropriate teaching methods, ensure you keep this in mind.

When using activities, you need to ensure they are inclusive and differentiate for individual learning styles and needs, learner difficulties and/or disabilities. Make sure your learners are aware *why* they are carrying out the activities and do not overcomplicate your sessions. When required, reasonable adjustments should be made to equipment and resources to ensure they are accessible to all.

At level 4, in addition to the above, you should read relevant textbooks, articles and journals, and access appropriate websites, referring to them in your response. When writing, you should be analytical rather than descriptive and use a recognised academic style of writing.

For example, you could compare and contrast theories regarding self-directed and active learning advocated by Knowles (2005) and Petty (2009). Both theorists identify that if your learners take the initiative and take charge of the direction of their learning, they will learn more things, learn better and achieve more. Petty (2009) identifies that it is important to develop your learners' thinking skills such as analysis, problem solving and evaluation. These are important transferable skills to develop in your learners which they should be able to use with confidence in various situations in their daily lives. You could further research this aspect of both theories and then reflect on how relevant this is to your learners.

Formal teaching is known as *pedagogy,* where the teacher directs all the learning. This method does not allow for individual learning styles to be taken into account. Teaching methods which focus on the learner are known as *andragogy,* for example group work and discussions. Knowles (2005) initially defined andragogy as *the art and science of helping adults learn.* An andragogical approach places more emphasis on what the learner is doing. Try and maximise the use of your learners' experiences by involving them whenever possible. Learners can learn from their peers' knowledge and experiences, as well as from you. Petty (2009) believes that we learn by doing. Active methods help learners use their learning in realistic and useful ways, and see its importance and relevance.

> Level 3 – 3.2 Identify the strengths and limitations of a range of resources, including new and emerging technologies, showing how these resources can be used to promote equality, support diversity and contribute to effective learning
>
> Level 4 – 3.2 Analyse the strengths and limitations of a range of resources, including new and emerging technologies, showing how these resources can be used to promote equality, support diversity and contribute to effective learning

Q24 Using a table similar to that below, identify a range of resources and state their strengths and limitations (include new and emerging technologies).

This is a practical task for you to complete a table identifying the range of resources you could use and what you consider are their strengths and limitations.

Table 3.1 Strengths and limitations of a range of resources

Resource	Strengths	Limitations
Websites	Help learners build their confidence and ability to use technology	Learners need to have access to the internet and basic computer skills Not all websites are accurate Makes plagiarism easy
Videos of taught sessions or learner activities	Can be uploaded to an intranet or VLE Learners can watch again in their own time to help them consolidate learning	Initial investment of time to create and produce Not all learners might want to participate
Real objects, for example clothing and items when teaching English for Speakers of Other Languages (ESOL)	Creating effective visual links between the item and the word, which enhances understanding	Having only one item may present a narrow view of what that word represents

Your table should include new and emerging technologies, for example using a discussion forum on a social networking site to support teaching and learning, using a Virtual Learning Environment (VLE) to upload handouts and assignments. You should also list all the other resources you use such as activities, books, digital cameras, flipcharts, handouts, interactive whiteboards, videos/DVDs, worksheets, etc.

At level 4, in addition to the above, you should read relevant textbooks, articles and journals, and access appropriate websites, referring to them in your response. When writing, you should be analytical rather than descriptive and use a recognised academic style of writing.

For example, you could access the Joint Information Systems Committee (JISC) website to gain inspiration in the use of innovation in new and emerging technologies in your specialist area. You could also research your relevant Sector Skills Council's website to find out which new and emerging technologies they support for your subject.

Q25 From the strengths and limitations identified in your table, analyse the overall contribution of each resource in terms of how they promote equality, support diversity and contribute to effective learning.

Using the *who, what, where, when, why* and *how* (wwwwwh) rationale is a good basis for determining how relevant, purposeful and effective your resource is. Take each resource you have listed in your table for question 24 and use the wwwwwh approach to state how they promote equality, support diversity and contribute to effective learning. For example, when accessing websites you might need to alter the background colours for those learners with dyslexia, which helps to promote equality, support diversity and contribute to effective learning. Always have a clear rationale to justify the resources you have chosen and evaluate them afterwards to help improve for the next time.

At level 4, in addition to the above, you should read relevant textbooks, articles and journals, and access appropriate websites, referring to them in your response. When writing, you should be analytical rather than descriptive and use a recognised academic style of writing.

For example, you could find out if there are any free resources available via the internet or if your colleagues have any you could use. Analyse one or two to see if they are appropriate for your subject. State what adjustments you would need to make to them to ensure they are inclusive, that they promote equality and diversity and that they meet the needs of your curriculum and learners.

> Level 3 – 3.3 Identify literacy, language, numeracy and ICT skills which are integral to own specialist area
>
> Level 4 –3.3 Identify literacy, language, numeracy and ICT skills which are integral to own specialist area, reviewing how they support learner achievement

Q26 Why is it important to assess the literacy, language, numeracy and ICT skills of your learners and how will embedding these in your programme support their achievement?

Your response should state how you identify the literacy, language, numeracy and ICT skills which are essential for your learners to successfully achieve their qualification or learning programme. You may feel that you need some support to do this and you should find out if you can work with someone in your organisation who is a specialist in these areas. Working with a literacy, language and numeracy specialist from the planning stages will help you to develop new approaches in embedding these skills within your subject. It will also help your learners to recognise the importance and value of these skills while learning. Improving these skills should help the employability prospects of your learners.

A thorough initial assessment should help identify the current skills and potential needs of your learners in these areas. You need to consider which aspects of these skills you want your learners to demonstrate within the context of their subject, for example the use of ICT skills when they are researching topics and using e-mail. It is important that the initial assessment tools are fit for purpose and will give the results needed to inform your learners' future plans.

Some learners may not have the required level of skills and knowledge and will therefore need to be referred for further guidance and support before commencing the programme. Improvements in their skills of literacy, language, numeracy and ICT will help support their subject learning and development.

Some examples of integrating the skills into your teaching and learning are:

- literacy – reading, writing, spelling, grammar, punctuation, syntax;

- language – speaking, listening, role play, interviews;

- numeracy – calculations, interpretations, evaluations, measurements;

- ICT – online learning, e-learning, word processing, use of a VLE, e-mails.

At level 4, in addition to the above, you should read relevant textbooks, articles and journals, and access appropriate websites, referring to them in your response. When writing, you should be analytical rather than descriptive and use a recognised academic style of writing.

For example, you could research the variety of terminology used (past and present) such as Basic Skills, Functional Skills, Key Skills, the Minimum Core and Skills for Life, stating the differences between them and why they were introduced.

You could read the document *Raising Standards: A Contextualised Guide to Support Success in Literacy, Numeracy and ESOL Provision* (Quality Improvement Agency for Lifelong Learning, 2008) which suggests carrying out a skills audit. You could carry out an audit of the literacy, language and numeracy skills of your learners which will pinpoint the specific level and type of skills needed to succeed. The audit could look at all the ways in which your learners have to use literacy, language and numeracy skills to follow the programme by examining:

- programme handouts and worksheets;

- textbooks and any standard reference books;

- the use of specialist formats for presenting text or numbers – reports, statistical tables, case studies, account ledgers, etc.;

- the use of specialist terminology and jargon;

- common teaching strategies, for example presentation, practical demonstration, simulation;

- the ways in which your learners are expected to record 'learning points' in sessions;

- private study tasks;

- group learning activities;

- assessment tasks (such as portfolio building), assessment criteria and feedback.

Q27 Using your current scheme of work and session plans, identify the opportunities for embedding and promoting literacy, language, numeracy and ICT skills and knowledge for your learners.

This is a practical task enabling you to identify the opportunities for literacy, language, numeracy and ICT skills within your teaching and learning resources. You could use a highlight pen to mark these on your documents and then write how you will embed them in practice during your sessions.

At level 4, in addition to the above, you should read relevant textbooks, articles and journals, and access appropriate websites, referring to them in your response. When writing, you should be analytical rather than descriptive and use a recognised academic style of writing.

You could create a direct cross reference from your scheme of work and session plans to your learner's individual learning plan. This will show evidence of the distance travelled and achievements in both the subject and the required literacy, language, numeracy and ICT skills. You could review the effectiveness of this approach in your reflective learning journal taking account of learner feedback.

> Level 3 – 3.4 Select/adapt and use a range of inclusive resources to promote inclusive learning and teaching
>
> Level 4 – 3.4 Select/adapt, use and justify a range of inclusive resources to promote inclusive learning and teaching

Q28 Justify your reasons for selecting, adapting and using your resources to promote inclusive learning and teaching.

This is a practical task enabling you to use a range of resources relevant to your subject area. Consider the resources you identified in the table you completed in question 24. Select and use some of these resources then add another column to the table to justify why you used them. You will need to consider your reasons for selecting a particular resource which may depend on the circumstances and needs of your learners. For example, you would not plan to use a website as a resource if you knew that the learning environment did not have internet access. The website might be the best resource to use; however, in these circumstances you would need to find a suitable alternative. In different circumstances, it would probably be more effective to use the website.

It is also important to think about whether a resource needs to be adapted so that all learners can use it. For example, if you have a learner who is visually impaired you would need to consider how you are going to prepare and use a resource so that it is accessible by this learner. This may mean using only a few words on each slide in an increased font size and simple font type. Your learner may need to sit closer to the screen and benefit from having a handout of all the slides printed in an enlarged font size.

At level 4, in addition to the above, you should read relevant textbooks, articles and journals, and access appropriate websites, referring to them in your response. When writing, you should be analytical rather than descriptive and use a recognised academic style of writing.

You could gain feedback from your learners to help you evaluate each resource used. This might give you some ideas of how you could adapt and improve them. If this is the case, once adapted, use them again to see how the improvements helped your learners. You could produce a case study showing the difference your resources made to the progress of your learners and how effective they were.

Theory focus

References and further information

Gould J (2009) *Learning Theory and Classroom Practice in the Lifelong Learning Sector*. Exeter: Learning Matters

Gravells A (2011) *Preparing to Teach in the Lifelong Learning Sector* (4th edition). Exeter: Learning Matters

Gravells A and Simpson S (2010) *Planning and Enabling in the Lifelong Learning Sector* (2nd edition). Exeter: Learning Matters

Hill C (2010) *Teaching with e-learning in the Lifelong Learning Sector* (2nd edition). Exeter: Learning Matters

Knowles M, Holton E and Swanson R (2005) *The adult learner: The Definitive Classic in Adult Education and Human Resource Development*. Oxford: Butterworth Heinemann

Laird D (2003) *Approaches to Training and Development* (3rd edition). New York: Basic Books

Petty G (2009) *Teaching Today* (4th edition). Cheltenham: Nelson Thornes

Quality Improvement Agency for Lifelong Learning (2008) *Raising Standards: A Contextualised Guide to Support Success in Literacy, Numeracy and ESOL Provision*.

Reece I and Walker S (2007) *Teaching, Training and Learning* (6th edition). Sunderland: Business Education Publishers Ltd

Wallace S (2007) *Managing Behaviour in the Lifelong Learning Sector* (2nd edition). Exeter: Learning Matters

Wallace S (2007) *Teaching, Training and Tutoring in the Lifelong Learning Sector* (3rd edition). Exeter: Learning Matters

Wilson L (2008) *Practical teaching: a guide to PTLLS and CTLLS*. London: Cengage Learning

Websites

JISC Inspiring Innovation – www.jisc.ac.uk

Motivation – tip.psychology.org/motivate.html

Raising Standards Guides – http://tinyurl.com/5ssozsd

Sector Skills Councils – www.sscalliance.org

Teaching and learning strategies – www.excellencegateway.org.uk/page.aspx?o=131034

Theories of learning – www.learningandteaching.info/learning/

Transforming the teaching and learning of Skills for Life – http://www.talent.ac.uk/content.asp?CategoryID=1892

CHAPTER 4
HOW TO USE A RANGE OF COMMUNICATION SKILLS AND METHODS TO COMMUNICATE EFFECTIVELY

This chapter is in two parts. The first part, **Self-assessment activities**, contains questions and activities which relate to the fourth learning outcome of the CTLLS mandatory unit: *Planning and Enabling Learning in the Lifelong Learning Sector – Understand how to use a range of communication skills and methods to communicate effectively with learners and relevant parties in own organisation.*

The assessment criteria for each level are shown in boxes and are followed by activities and questions for you to carry out. Ensure your responses are *specific to you*, the *subject* you will teach and the *context* and *environment* in which you will teach.

After completing the activities and questions, check your responses with the second part: **Guidance for evidencing competence**. This guidance is not intended to give you the answers to questions you may be asked in any formal assessments; however, it will help you focus your responses towards meeting the CTLLS requirements.

Self-assessment activities

Level 3 – 4.1 Use different communication methods and skills to meet the needs of learners and the organisation

Level 4 – 4.1 Use and evaluate different communication methods and skills to meet the needs of learners and the organisation

Q29 Describe the different communication methods and skills you could use with your learners and colleagues.

Q30 How can the communication methods and skills meet the needs of your learners and your organisation?

Q31 Use and evaluate different communication methods and skills.

Level 3 – 4.2 Identify ways in which own communication skills could be improved, including an explanation of how barriers to effective communication might be overcome

Level 4 – 4.2 Evaluate own communication skills, identifying ways in which these could be improved including an analysis of how barriers to effective communication might be overcome

Q32 What barriers might there be to effective communication and how could these be overcome?

Q33 Analyse the ways in which you currently communicate and identify how your own communication skills could be improved.

Level 3 – 4.3 Liaise with other relevant parties to effectively meet the needs of learners

Level 4 – 4.3 Identify and liaise with appropriate and relevant parties to effectively meet the needs of learners

Q34 Who are the other relevant parties you would liaise with to effectively meet the needs of your learners?

Q35 Liaise with these parties to effectively meet the needs of your learners.

Guidance for evidencing competence

Level 3 – 4.1 Use different communication methods and skills to meet the needs of learners and the organisation

Level 4 – 4.1 Use and evaluate different communication methods and skills to meet the needs of learners and the organisation

Q29 Describe the different communication methods and skills you could use with your learners and colleagues.

Your response should describe what communication is, i.e. a means of passing on information from one person to another. It is the key to encouraging learner motivation, managing behaviour and disruption, promoting good working relationships, and becoming a successful and professional teacher. Communication methods include verbal, non-verbal and written, and can be formal or informal. These methods are constantly evolving due to new and emerging technologies. For example, e-mails, text messages, podcasts, webcasts, internet forums, chat rooms and VLEs.

Communication is also a manner of expression, for example body language, tone of voice and gestures. Body language includes facial expressions, eye contact, posture and appearance. You need to be aware not only of your own body language, but also that of your learners; you need to sense what they are not saying as well as what they are saying. Always check your learners have understood what you have communicated. Never assume they have received and interpreted it the way you intended as they may have misheard, misread or misinterpreted something. Whether you are communicating formally, i.e. when teaching or in a meeting, or informally, i.e. chatting to a colleague or using e-mail, you should always remain professional and act with integrity and respect.

Communication will be internal, i.e. with colleagues within your organisation, or external, i.e. with people such as employers or parents.

Communication skills are the ways in which you apply the different communication methods, for example speaking, listening, reading and writing, all of which you will need to demonstrate in practice.

- Speaking – the way you converse with others, how you use questioning techniques, maintain attention and how you give feedback; how you act, i.e. remaining professional at all times; how assertive and confident you are; the language, amount of technical jargon you use and ambiguity; the way you project your voice and use inflection and tone; knowing when to use pauses to gain attention or allow thinking time; speaking clearly and slightly louder and slower than normal, being aware of dialect and accents and considering others whose first language is not English; being conscious of how you speak differently to individuals as opposed to groups.

- Listening – using eye contact, gestures, facial expressions, posture and non-verbal signals to show you are listening; not deliberately interrupting, being judgemental or argumentative; knowing when to be sympathetic or empathic.

- Reading – interpreting and comprehending written information from various sources such as learners' work, journals, textbooks, the internet, etc.; recognising when to speed read, skim or scan text for key points.

- Writing – creating presentations, handouts, worksheets, writing feedback and progress reports, making legible and accessible notes, completing forms, etc.; checking your spelling, grammar, punctuation and sentence construction, the tone in which you are writing and the suitability of the level of language to the reader.

These four skills are part of the minimum core of literacy, language, numeracy and ICT (see Chapter 13 for more information).

The language you use should reflect equality and inclusiveness, be relevant to the subject, not offend anyone in any way and be pitched at an appropriate level for your learners. Learning occurs best in an active, not a passive environment where communication is a two-way process. Always watch for signals from your learners to check they are learning.

Effective listening only takes place when the person who receives the information interprets and understands it the way the deliverer intended. It can be easy to say something and think you said it in a way that your learners will understand, only to find them asking you to say it again or to rephrase it.

At level 4, in addition to the above, you should read relevant textbooks, articles and journals, and access appropriate websites, referring to them in your response. When writing, you should be analytical rather than descriptive and use a recognised academic style of writing.

For example, you could evaluate why people behave differently in group situations or when part of a team. Belbin (2010) defined team roles as *a tendency to behave, contribute and interrelate with others at work in certain distinctive ways* (p24).

You could review Belbin's research and compare it to others such as Coverdale (1977). He argued that the essence of team working is that individuals have their own preferred ways of achieving a task, but that in a team, they need to decide on one way of achieving this. Another communication theorist is Tuckman (1965) who argues that *individuals in groups go through various stages from when they meet to when they complete the task.*

Q30 How can the communication methods and skills meet the needs of your learners and your organisation?

Your response should include examples of learner and organisational needs and how they can be met. For example, learners taking a distance learning programme will need to access information and materials electronically via a VLE, or traditionally via a postal service. They will probably communicate by e-mail, webcam, an online forum, telephone or post.

All learners should have the opportunity to learn in a safe and comfortable environment, and should be treated with respect. Agreeing ground rules with your learners will help them to be aware of the boundaries within which to work and lead to improved communication, for example not interrupting someone when they are speaking and respecting others' opinions.

Once you get to know your learners and their learning styles, you will be able to communicate with them in ways to support their learning, for example paraphrasing or rephrasing sentences, holding discussions, facilitating role plays and encouraging oral questions.

You might have some situations, for example a learner with a concern about their assignment, which would benefit from a face-to-face conversation rather than an electronic or telephone communication. Team meetings might take place in person or via a webcam if staff are based at different locations. Writing a letter to a learner is a more formal approach if they have several pieces of outstanding work. A written record of a tutorial review would leave your learner with a document they can refer to afterwards. All communication methods should be appropriate to the situation and the person, and take into account social, regional and cultural differences.

At level 4, in addition to the above, you should read relevant textbooks, articles and journals, and access appropriate websites, referring to them in your response. When writing, you should be analytical rather than descriptive and use a recognised academic style of writing.

For example, you could refer to Maslow's (1954) Hierarchy of Needs. He argued that there are five needs which represent different levels of motivation which must be met. These are: physiological; safety and security; recognition, self-esteem and self-actualisation. If you can communicate with your learners in a way that meets these needs, you will be helping them to progress through the levels.

Q31 Use and evaluate different communication methods and skills.

This is a practical task which enables you to use different communication methods and skills. As part of the CTLLS programme, you will be observed at some point by your assessor. They will make notes regarding how you communicate with your learners. You should also maintain a reflective learning journal, and/or complete a self-evaluation form analysing how effective your communication methods and skills are.

At level 4, in addition to the above, you should read relevant textbooks, articles and journals, and access appropriate websites, referring to them in your response. When writing, you should be analytical rather than descriptive and use a recognised academic style of writing.

For example, you could evaluate why you used particular communication methods and skills for different situations, such as formal or informal, verbal or written. You could make a visual or audio recording of you communicating with others and after watching it, evaluate the process and make recommendations regarding what you would do differently next time.

You might like to refer to Chapter 5 of Gravells and Simpson (2010) *Planning and Enabling Learning in the Lifelong Learning Sector*, which contains checklists for effective communication.

> Level 3 – 4.2 Identify ways in which own communication skills could be improved, including an explanation of how barriers to effective communication might be overcome
>
> Level 4 – 4.2 Evaluate own communication skills, identifying ways in which these could be improved including an analysis of how barriers to effective communication might be overcome

Q32 What barriers might there be to effective communication and how could these be overcome?

Barriers to effective communication can be internal, i.e. people's attitudes, behaviour, emotions, motivation and thoughts. They can also be external, i.e. the culture, environment, peer pressure and the type of language used.

Your response might include some of the following barriers:

- attendance, i.e. irregularity;
- background noise and interruptions;
- behavioural difficulties;
- culture, i.e. why things are done in a certain way or people behave in a certain manner;
- discipline, i.e. issues impacting upon attention;
- distractions, i.e. aural and/or visual;
- hearing or visual impairment;
- lack of confidence, interest and/or motivation;
- lack of contact, i.e. learners taking a distance learning programme;
- lack of or limited access to communication equipment, i.e. e-mail, computer, telephone, etc.;
- lack of prior knowledge and/or experience;

- lack of privacy for confidential conversations;

- language problems, i.e. level pitched too low or high, amount of technical jargon used, English as a second language;

- learning difficulties and disabilities;

- limited basic skills such as literacy, numeracy and ICT;

- mixed ability learning styles;

- personal/work/home circumstances;

- physical, medical, mental or health conditions;

- poor questioning skills;

- position, i.e. can everyone fully see and hear;

- pressures, i.e. the amount of time you have;

- previous experiences impacting upon current situation;

- resources, i.e. not enough for everyone or too difficult to interpret and use;

- the environment, i.e. too cold to concentrate, seating arrangements;

- the listener or reader not interpreting the information the way it was intended;

- the speaker's voice, i.e. accent, dialect, pace, tone and volume;

- social skills, i.e. inability to concentrate for long periods;

- writing skills, i.e. illegible.

Your response should address how you would deal with each point you have listed as a barrier. To overcome these you need to ensure you communicate in an effective way which suits the people you are with and the situation you are in at the time. For example, when teaching you should make sure all your learners can see and hear you, that you use language at an appropriate level for their understanding, and that any written materials are legible and accessible to all.

You might also have barriers yourself, for example you might plan to introduce a complex or emotive topic to your learners, which could be misinterpreted if not conveyed logically or sensitively. You might not be aware of your body language, for example constantly fiddling with a pen or waving your arms when speaking. Your voice projection might not be strong enough to reach everyone, and/or resources and handouts you produce might have spelling errors. If you speak too quickly or give too much factual information too soon, your learners will not have time to assimilate their new knowledge.

At level 4, in addition to the above, you should read relevant textbooks, articles and journals, and access appropriate websites, referring to them in your response. When writing, you should be analytical rather than descriptive and use a recognised academic style of writing.

For example, you could evaluate your current personal communication styles. You may have to adapt the way you communicate to suit the needs of others, as how they see and hear you may be different to the way you intended. You could research Berne's (2010) *Transactional Analysis* theory which he created in 1961 and is a method of analysing communications between people. Berne identified three personality states; the *child*, the *parent* and the *adult*. These states are called *ego states* and people behave and exist in a mixture of these states depending on their past experiences and the situation at the time, and this affects their gestures, vocal tones, expressions, attitudes and vocabulary. You could analyse why you, your colleagues or your learners behave differently depending upon who they are with and the situation they are in.

Q33 Analyse the ways in which you currently communicate and identify how your own communication skills could be improved.

The ways in which you currently communicate will probably include verbal (speaking to individuals and groups in person or via an electronic method), non-verbal (your image and the way you act) and written (by hand, electronically, etc.). When analysing these you need to consider how well you communicate and why. This will be dependent upon the situation and whether it was formal or informal.

To identify how your communication skills could be improved involves recognising that they need to be improved. Feedback from your learners, mentor, colleagues, inspectors and verifiers can help. For example, if your learners are looking confused when you are talking to them, they probably have not understood what you were asking or saying. If a colleague does not do something you asked them to, they might have misinterpreted your request. Being aware of the ways in which you communicate with others will help you realise the need to improve and then you can do something about it to become more effective.

Your response should give examples of how you could improve:

● ensuring inclusivity of all learners and addressing differentiation, equality and diversity during each session;

● improving your writing skills, i.e. spelling, grammar and punctuation;

● making sure the environment and all resources are appropriate;

● managing behaviour, disruptions and group activities effectively;

● managing own emotions;

● practising your speaking and listening skills;

● rephrasing questions;

● researching different ways of asking questions;

● taking further training in relevant topics to suit your job role;

- taking time to find out about the people you will be communicating with, their background and prior knowledge and experience;

- using formal and informal communication methods appropriately;

- using ICT to its best effect;

- using more eye contact;

- using non-verbal communication to good effect.

At level 4, in addition to the above, you should read relevant textbooks, articles and journals, and access appropriate websites, referring to them in your response. When writing, you should be analytical rather than descriptive and use a recognised academic style of writing.

For example, you could evaluate how your own communication skills could be improved by discussing relevant quotes such as Appleyard and Appleyard (2010).

> In addition to your own idea of how to communicate at work, the organisation as a whole has expectations as to how you will do your job; so do all the people you communicate with. Problems tend to arise when these expectations are not met and this can be reflected in the communication process.

> (p101)

You could also evaluate how the expectations of others you communicate with have an impact upon the way you communicate, giving examples of how you could improve. You could create an action plan for yourself to achieve your identified improvements, with appropriate target dates for completion. You could also complete a reflective learning journal giving examples of communication situations.

Level 3 – 4.3 Liaise with other relevant parties to effectively meet the needs of learners

Level 4 – 4.3 Identify and liaise with appropriate and relevant parties to effectively meet the needs of learners

---

Q34 Who are the other relevant parties you would liaise with to effectively meet the needs of your learners?

Other relevant parties will include internal and external persons and agencies such as:

- counsellors;

- employers;

- examination officers;

- external agencies such as banks, Citizens Advice Bureaux, employment agencies, etc.;

- careers advisers;

- internal and external moderators and verifiers;

- interpreters;

- learners;

- learning support staff;

- line managers or supervisors;

- parents, carers and guardians;

- teachers and administrative staff;

- workplace witnesses.

It would be helpful if you know the name of the relevant person and their contact details to be able to respond effectively to meet any needs as they arise.

At level 4, in addition to the above, you should read relevant textbooks, articles and journals, and access appropriate websites, referring to them in your response. When writing, you should be analytical rather than descriptive and use a recognised academic style of writing.

For example, you could give an instance of how you would liaise with each party you have listed for a particular reason. You could obtain information such as the name of a suitable contact, their telephone number, and address and/or website details. This way, you will be prepared for when you need to communicate with them. You could also state how you will communicate, i.e. formally or informally and under what circumstances it would occur.

Q35 Liaise with these parties to effectively meet the needs of your learners.

This is a practical task enabling you to demonstrate and evidence how you liaise with others to effectively meet the needs of your learners. For example, you might have a learner whose writing skills need improving. You could therefore liaise with staff internally in your own organisation to arrange learning support, or refer them to an external agency for further training. You will need to provide evidence to prove you have liaised with others such as audio recordings, e-mails, feedback from others, letters, telephone messages, etc. Do maintain appropriate confidentiality of your learners throughout the liaison process and discuss these instances with your assessor if you cannot provide physical evidence. Your assessor might also observe you liaising with others at some point.

At level 4, in addition to the above, you should read relevant textbooks, articles and journals, and access appropriate websites, referring to them in your response. When writing, you should be analytical rather than descriptive and use a recognised academic style of writing.

For example, you could evaluate why you liaised with the parties that you did, what the benefit was to the learner and how you might do things differently next time.

Theory focus

References and further information

Appleyard N and Appleyard K (2010) *Communicating with learners in the Lifelong Learning Sector.* Exeter: Learning Matters

Belbin M (2010) *Team Roles At Work* (2nd edition). Oxford: Butterworth-Heinemann

Berne E (2010) *Games People Play: The Psychology of Human Relationships.* London: Penguin Books Ltd

Coverdale R (1977) *Risk Thinking.* Bradford: The Coverdale Organisation

Gravells A and Simpson S (2010) *Planning and Enabling Learning in the Lifelong Learning Sector.* Exeter: Learning Matters

Maslow A (1954) *Motivation and Personality.* New York: Harper

Tuckman B (1965) Developmental sequence in small groups. *Psychological bulletin,* 63: 384–99

Wallace S (2007) *Managing Behaviour in the Lifelong Learning Sector* (2nd edition). Exeter: Learning Matters.

Websites

Accessibility in Learning – www.excellencegateway.org.uk/page.aspx?o=jisctechdis

Functional Skills – www.qcda.gov.uk/qualifications/30.aspx

Tuckman's team development –www.businessballs.com/tuckmanformingstorming normingperforming.htm

CHAPTER 5
THE MINIMUM CORE IN OWN PRACTICE

This chapter is in two parts. The first part, *Self-assessment activities*, contains questions and activities which relate to the fifth learning outcome of the CTLLS mandatory unit: *Planning and Enabling Learning in the Lifelong Learning Sector – Understand and demonstrate knowledge of the minimum core in own practice.*

The assessment criteria for each level are shown in boxes and are followed by activities and questions for you to carry out. Ensure your responses are *specific to you*, the *subject* you will teach and the *context* and *environment* in which you will teach.

After completing the activities and questions, check your responses with the second part: *Guidance for evidencing competence*. This guidance is not intended to give you the answers to questions you may be asked in any formal assessments; however, it will help you focus your responses towards meeting the CTLLS requirements.

Self-assessment activities

Please see Chapter 13 for background information regarding the minimum core.

> Level 3 – 5.1 Apply minimum core specifications in literacy to improve own practice
>
> Level 3 – 5.2 Apply minimum core specifications in language to improve own practice
>
> Level 4 – 5.1 Apply minimum core specifications in literacy to improve own practice
>
> Level 4 – 5.2 Apply minimum core specifications in language to improve own practice

Q36 How can you apply the minimum core specifications in literacy and language?

> Level 3 – 5.3 Apply minimum core specifications in numeracy to improve own practice
>
> Level 4 – 5.3 Apply minimum core specifications in numeracy to improve own practice

Q37 How can you apply the minimum core specifications in numeracy?

Level 3 – 5.4 Apply minimum core specifications in ICT user skills to improve own practice

Level 4 – 5.4 Apply minimum core specifications in ICT user skills to improve own practice

Q38 How can you apply the minimum core specifications in ICT user skills?

Guidance for evidencing competence

Please see Chapter 13 for background information regarding the minimum core.

> Level 3 – 5.1 Apply minimum core specifications in literacy to improve own practice
>
> Level 3 – 5.2 Apply minimum core specifications in language to improve own practice
>
> Level 4 – 5.1 Apply minimum core specifications in literacy to improve own practice
>
> Level 4 – 5.2 Apply minimum core specifications in language to improve own practice

Q36 How can you apply the minimum core specifications in literacy and language?

Your response should state how you apply aspects of literacy and language while teaching your specialist subject. For example, when preparing programme materials such as handouts and presentations, you should ensure your spelling and punctuation are correct. If there are errors or mistakes, then your learners may think it is right when it is not. You could explain how important it is to plan for the appropriate use and level of literacy and language based on your understanding of the different attitudes and expectations of your learners. You could focus on the language skills required in occupations related to your specialist area and thus prepare your learners better for employment.

You should have knowledge about language and of the four skills of speaking, listening, reading and writing, and be able to show you understand these by putting them into practice. Demonstrating your personal skills will be shown by the way you communicate with your learners (written, verbal and non-verbal), how you respond to situations and give feedback, what reference and support materials you use and how your convey your literacy, i.e. using accurate spelling, grammar and punctuation in written text. Evidence you could provide includes your scheme of work, session plans, activities you have designed for learners, resource materials, handouts and presentations.

At level 4, in addition to the above, you should read relevant textbooks, articles and journals, and access appropriate websites, referring to them in your response. When writing, you should be analytical rather than descriptive and use a recognised academic style of writing.

For example, you could review the LLUK documents (2007a, 2007b) and analyse the aspects of the literacy and language that you can demonstrate within your teaching. You could then review the impact upon your learners due to your increased knowledge and understanding, and produce an action plan for your own development. You may feel your literacy and language skills need improving; if so, you could access the www.move-on.org.uk website and complete the activities which will contribute to the National Literacy Test at level 2 – an acceptable quali-fication to demonstrate the minimum core achievement in this area.

You could improve your own practice by researching your subject area to bring yourself up to date with specialist language, terminology and jargon. You could then use this knowledge during your teaching and in any resources you use with your learners.

> Level 3 – 5.3 Apply minimum core specifications in numeracy to improve own practice
>
> Level 4 – 5.3 Apply minimum core specifications in numeracy to improve own practice

Q37 How can you apply the minimum core specifications in numeracy?

Your response should state how you apply aspects of numeracy while teaching your specialist subject. For example, when preparing teaching and learning activ-ities, use aspects which develop your own numerical knowledge. You will need to embed the Functional Skill of maths during your teaching and not make any assumptions that your learners know how to carry out numerical calculations. Besides evidencing your own numerical skills, you should show that you are sup-porting your learners' skills. For example, if your learners are studying to be carpet fitters and they do not know how to work out the area of a room then this will have an impact on their progress and achievement. If your own numerical skills are up to standard, then you will be able to support your learners.

You should have knowledge about numerical communication and processes and be able to show you understand these by putting them into practice. Demonstrating your personal skills will be shown by how you communicate with others regard-ing numeracy (to support your teaching role and your learners' understanding), and how you use processes such as analysing data, making calculations and solving problems. Evidence you could provide includes statistical analysis, reports, reten-tion, achievement and success data, and financial calculations.

At level 4, in addition to the above, you should read relevant textbooks, articles and journals, and access appropriate websites, referring to them in your response. When writing, you should be analytical rather than descriptive and use a recog-nised academic style of writing.

For example, you could review the LLUK documents (2007a, 2007b) and anal-yse the aspects of numeracy that you can demonstrate within your teaching. You could then review the impact upon your learners of your increased knowledge and understanding, and produce an action plan for your own development. You may feel your numerical skills need improving; if so, you could access the www.move-on.org.uk website and complete the activities which will contribute to the National Numeracy Test at level 2 – an acceptable qualification to demonstrate the mini-mum core achievement in this area.

Level 3 – 5.4 Apply minimum core specifications in ICT user skills to improve own practice

Level 4 – 5.4 Apply minimum core specifications in ICT user skills to improve own practice

Q38 How can you apply the minimum core specifications in ICT user skills?

Your response should state how you apply aspects of ICT while teaching your specialist subject. You could use various aspects of ICT, for example, a VLE, an interactive whiteboard, accessing video clips, using e-mail and carrying out research via the internet.

You should have knowledge about ICT and processes and be able to show you understand these by putting them into practice. Demonstrating your personal skills will be shown by how you communicate with others in a variety of ways and how you use ICT systems to support teaching and learning. Evidence you could provide includes practical examples of using ICT such as e-mails, presentation equipment, software packages, a VLE and documents you have produced electronically such as handouts or interactive activities.

At level 4, in addition to the above, you should read relevant textbooks, articles and journals, and access appropriate websites, referring to them in your response. When writing, you should be analytical rather than descriptive and use a recognised academic style of writing.

For example, you could research new and emerging technologies in your specialist subject area via your specialist subject Sector Skills Council or JISC and then reflect on what the impact would be if you integrated their use into your teaching and learning.

You could review the LLUK documents (2007a, 2007b) and analyse the aspects of ICT that you can demonstrate within your teaching. You could then review the impact upon your learners of your increased knowledge and understanding, and produce an action plan for your own development. You may feel your ICT skills need improving; if so, you could access the www.onlinebasics.co.uk website and complete the activities to give you more confidence at using the basics of ICT. You could then research other online courses to increase your knowledge and skills and consider taking a relevant ICT qualification.

Theory focus

References and further information

Appleyard N and Appleyard K (2009) *The Minimum Core for Numeracy: Knowledge, Understanding and Personal Skills.* Exeter: Learning Matters

Clarke A (2009) *The Minimum Core for Information and Communication Technology: Knowledge, Understanding and Personal Skills.* Exeter: Learning Matters

LLUK (2007a) *Addressing literacy, language, numeracy and ICT needs in education and training: Defining the minimum core of teachers' knowledge, understanding and personal skills.* London: Lifelong Learning UK

LLUK (2007b) *Literacy, Language, Numeracy and ICT: Inclusive learning approaches for all teachers, tutors and trainers in the learning and skills sector.* London: Lifelong Learning UK

Peart S (2009) *The Minimum Core for Numeracy: Knowledge, Understanding and Personal Skills.* Exeter: Learning Matters

Websites

English and maths online tests (free) – www.move-on.org.uk

Functional Skills – www.qcda.gov.uk/qualifications/30.aspx

ICT online course (free) – www.onlinebasics.co.uk

Joint Information Systems Committee – www.jisc.ac.uk/

Minimum Core Standards – tinyurl.com/6zmwcg

CHAPTER 6
HOW REFLECTION, EVALUATION AND FEEDBACK CAN BE USED TO DEVELOP OWN PRACTICE

This chapter is in two parts. The first part, *Self-assessment activities*, contains questions and activities which relate to the sixth learning outcome of the CTLLS mandatory unit: *Planning and Enabling Learning in the Lifelong Learning Sector – Understand how reflection, evaluation and feedback can be used to develop own practice.*

The assessment criteria for each level are shown in boxes and are followed by activities and questions for you to carry out. Ensure your responses are *specific to you*, the *subject* you will teach and the *context* and *environment* in which you will teach.

After completing the activities and questions, check your responses with the second part: *Guidance for evidencing competence*. This guidance is not intended to give you the answers to questions you may be asked in any formal assessments; however, it will help you focus your responses towards meeting the CTLLS requirements.

Self-assessment activities

Level 3 – 6.1 Use regular reflection and feedback from others, including learners, to evaluate and improve own practice

Level 4 – 6.1 Use regular reflection and feedback from others, including learners, to evaluate and improve own practice, making recommendations for modification as appropriate

Q39 Reflect on the effectiveness of your own practice as a teacher.

Q40 How can you obtain the views of others, including your learners, regarding the teaching and learning process?

Q41 How can you improve your own practice as a result of your reflection and the feedback you have obtained?

Guidance for evidencing competence

Level 3 – 6.1 Use regular reflection and feedback from others, including learners, to evaluate and improve own practice

Level 4 – 6.1 Use regular reflection and feedback from others, including learners, to evaluate and improve own practice, making recommendations for modification as appropriate

Q39 Reflect on the effectiveness of your own practice as a teacher.

To reflect or evaluate the effectiveness of your practice as a teacher, you need to consider your role throughout the whole process of the teaching and learning cycle.

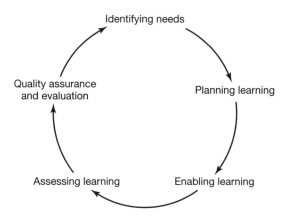

Figure 6.1 The teaching and learning cycle

Your response should include examples of your experiences and reflections regarding your effectiveness as a teacher, for example:

- identifying needs – how you ensured this process was effective for your learners, yourself and the organisation;

- planning learning – how your scheme of work, session plans and resources ensured teaching and learning were effective;

- enabling learning – how the teaching and learning approaches you used were effective;

- assessing learning – how the assessment process was effective for your learners, yourself and the organisation;

- quality assurance and evaluation – how you obtained feedback from others, and evaluated yourself and the programme in order to make improvements for the future.

Reflection involves self-evaluation and taking into account feedback from others such as your line manager and mentor, colleagues, learners and their supervisors, if applicable. You have a professional accountability towards your organisation and your learners, as well as all the stakeholders involved in the teaching and learning process. These could include external bodies responsible for funding and inspections, and your learners' employers if applicable. You should also be following the Code of Professional Practice (Institute for Learning, 2009).

There may be procedures within your organisation to help you reflect and evaluate, for example an appraisal or review system with your line manager, learner questionnaires and learner surveys. The feedback you gain from these will help you consider how effective you are.

You have probably been writing a reflective learning journal throughout your time taking the CTLLS qualification and this will provide evidence towards this activity. When reflecting or writing your journal, it is best to have the *experience*, then *describe it, analyse it* and *revise it* (EDAR). This method should help you think about what has happened and then consider ways of changing and/or improving it.

Experience → Describe → Analyse → Revise
EDAR

- *Experience* – a significant event or incident you would like to change or improve.

- *Describe* – aspects such as *who* was involved, *what* happened, *when* it happened and *where* it happened.

- *Analyse* – consider the experience further and ask yourself *how* it happened and *why* it happened.

- *Revise* – think about *how* you would do it differently if it happened again and then try this out if you have the opportunity.

As part of your response to this question, you could work through each of the EDAR points to reflect upon your role as a teacher for each stage of the teaching and learning cycle.

At level 4, in addition to the above, you should read relevant textbooks, articles and journals, and access appropriate websites, referring to them in your response. When writing, you should be analytical rather than descriptive and use a recognised academic style of writing.

For example, you could evaluate the effectiveness of your practice through each stage of the teaching and learning cycle by relating to reflective theorists such as: Brookfield (1995), Gibbs (1988), Griffiths and Tann (1992), Kolb (1984), Schön (1983) and others. You could also compare and contrast the different theories.

Q40 How can you obtain the views of others, including your learners, regarding the teaching and learning process?

Obtaining the views of others will greatly assist you when reflecting upon your role as a teacher as well as the learning process. Your response should include how you can obtain feedback from others, including your learners. Examples might include appraisals, discussions, questionnaires, observations, reviews and surveys, whether formal or informal, paper-based or electronic.

Formal feedback can come from questionnaires, surveys, open questions to individuals or groups (in person, online, telephone, text, etc.), comment cards or even complaints and appeals. Feedback can be gained anonymously, in which case you will probably receive more information if learners do not have to disclose their name. Your organisation might have standard questionnaires or surveys you are required to use, or you could design your own. If necessary, build time into your session for these to take place; otherwise your learners may take away the questionnaire and forget to return it. You might also take part in an appraisal process at your organisation and gain feedback through this, or you might receive verbal and written feedback from others, such as your colleagues, mentor, line manager, learners, and their employers if applicable.

When evaluating this feedback, you should use it to improve your own performance, the support you give your learners, and the full teaching and learning process. You could gain feedback from your learners after trying something new or unfamiliar, for example using new technology during a session. Never assume everything is going well just because you think it is. Encouraging your learners to talk to you about anything you can do to help them, or things you can change to support their learning, will help build a climate of trust and respect.

When designing questionnaires, you need to be careful of the type of questions you are asking, and consider why you are asking them. Do not just ask a question for the sake of it; consider what you really want to find out. When writing questions, ensure the language and level you use suits your learners. You will also need to consider whether your questions will be *closed*, i.e. a question only requiring a *yes* or *no* answer, *multiple choice*, i.e. enabling your learner to choose one or more responses to a question, or *open*, leading to detailed factual responses.

If you use closed or multiple choice questions this will make analysis easy as you can just add up how many of each response you received; this is known as *quantitative* data. Other responses will give you *qualitative* data. Quantitative data is useful for obtaining statistics, but will not give you much information to help you improve specific aspects of the teaching and learning process. Although you can add up the responses quickly from quantitative data, qualitative data is more useful. You might find it best to use a mixture of open and closed questions. When designing questionnaires, use the KISS method – **K**eep **I**t **S**hort and **S**imple. Do not overcomplicate your questions, i.e. by asking two questions in one sentence or by making the questionnaire so long that your learners will not want to complete it.

At level 4, in addition to the above, you should read relevant textbooks, articles and journals, and access appropriate websites, referring to them in your response. When writing, you should be analytical rather than descriptive and use a recognised academic style of writing.

For example, you could refer to different ways of producing and analysing questionnaires, referencing your response to various theorists such as Cohen et al (2007) and Denscombe (2002).

You could also provide evidence of questionnaires or surveys you have used with your learners, along with a summary of the responses and any action required.

Q41 How can you improve your own practice as a result of your reflection and the feedback you have obtained?

Your response should take into consideration your own reflections and the feedback you have gained from others. While you might consider your current practice is effective, there will possibly be areas you could improve upon. As part of your response, you could go through each stage of the teaching and learning cycle (see Figure 6.1) in question 39, stating what you could do to improve your practice.

For example, feedback from learners might have stated that the initial assessment process was rather rushed as it took place during the first session. You could therefore arrange for this process to be carried out prior to your learners commencing, for example at the interview stage or by using new technology to enable learners to complete it online.

Improving your own practice should help improve your confidence and lead to an improvement in your learners' progress and achievement. It should also ensure you are up to date with changes and developments regarding your specialist subject and teaching in general.

Improving your own practice is not just about making changes to what you do. It includes carrying out CPD to ensure you are up to date regarding developments with your subject and with teaching and learning in general. You could consider your strengths and limitations and create a SMART action plan for your further development. You could reflect upon relevant CPD you have completed, submitting your reflections of these as evidence. It is a requirement that all teachers register with the IfL, maintain their CPD, submit an annual declaration by August of each year and follow the Code of Professional Practice (Institute for Learning, 2009).

At level 4, in addition to the above, you should read relevant textbooks, articles and journals, and access appropriate websites, referring to them in your response. When writing, you should be analytical rather than descriptive and use a recognised academic style of writing.

For example, you could refer to a relevant quote such as the following from the IfL, and explain how you will meet their requirements.

The activities you choose as relevant to you and your practice will only count as CPD if:

● *you can critically reflect on what you have learned;*

● *you can evidence how you have applied this to your practice;*

● *you can evidence how this has impacted on your learners' experience and success.*

(Institute for Learning, 2007, p10)

You could also carry out a SWOT analysis (strengths, weaknesses, opportunities and threats) regarding your practice as a teacher.

Theory focus

References and further information

Brookfield S (1995) *Becoming a Critically Reflective Teacher.* San Francisco: Jossey Bass

Cohen L, Manion L and Morrison K (2007) *Research Methods in Education.* London: Routledge

Denscombe M (2002) *Ground Rules for Good Research.* Buckingham: Open University Press

Gibbs G (1988) *Learning by doing: a guide to teaching and learning methods.* Oxford: Further Education Unit

Gravells A and Simpson S (2010) *Planning and Enabling Learning in the Lifelong Learning Sector* (2nd edition). Exeter: Learning Matters

Griffiths M and Tann S (1992) Using reflective practice to link personal and public theories. *Journal of Education for Teaching,* 18(1)

Hitching J (2008) *Maintaining Your Licence to Practise.* Exeter: Learning Matters

Institute for Learning (2007) *Guidelines for Continuing Professional Development.* London: IfL

Institute for Learning (2009) *Code of Professional Practice: Raising concerns about IfL members* (V2). London: IfL

Kolb D (1984) *Experiential Learning: Experience as the Source of Learning and Development.* New Jersey: Prentice-Hall

Roffey-Barentsen J and Malthouse R (2009) *Reflective Practice in the Lifelong Learning Sector.* Exeter: Learning Matters

Schön D (1983) *The Reflective Practitioner.* San Francisco: Jossey-Bass

Tummons J (2011) *Becoming a Professional Tutor in the Lifelong Learning Sector* (3rd edition). Exeter: Learning Matters

Wallace S and Gravells J (2007) *Mentoring.* Exeter: Learning Matters

Wood J and Dickinson J (2011) *Quality Assurance and Evaluation in the Lifelong Learning Sector.* Exeter: Learning Matters

Websites

Institute for Learning – www.ifl.ac.uk

Reflective practice – www.learningandteaching.info/learning/reflecti.htm

SWOT analysis – www.businessballs.com/swotanalysisfreetemplate.htm

CHAPTER 7
KEY CONCEPTS AND PRINCIPLES
OF ASSESSMENT

This chapter is in two parts. The first part, *Self-assessment activities*, contains questions and activities which relate to the first learning outcome of the CTLLS mandatory unit: *Principles and Practice of Assessment in the Lifelong Learning Sector – Understand key concepts and principles of assessment.*

The assessment criteria for each level are shown in boxes and are followed by activities and questions for you to carry out. Ensure your responses are *specific to you*, the *subject* you will teach and the *context* and *environment* in which you will teach.

After completing the activities and questions, check your responses with the second part: *Guidance for evidencing competence*. This guidance is not intended to give you the answers to questions you may be asked in any formal assessments; however, it will help you focus your responses towards meeting the CTLLS requirements.

Self-assessment activities

> Level 3 – 1.1 Identify and define the key concepts and principles of assessment
>
> Level 4 –1.1 Summarise the key concepts and principles of assessment

Q42 What is assessment, why should it take place and when does it happen?

Q43 What is the role of an assessor?

Q44 What is an assessment strategy and why have one?

Q45 Identify the key concepts of assessment.

Q46 Summarise the key principles of assessment.

Guidance for evidencing competence

Level 3 – 1.1 Identify and define the key concepts and principles of assessment

Level 4 – 1.1 Summarise the key concepts and principles of assessment

Q42 What is assessment, why should it take place and when does it happen?

Your response should state that assessment is a way of finding out if learning has taken place. It should confirm each learner's progress and achievement at a given point towards their programme or qualification. It can also confirm, through initial assessment, the starting point for a programme of learning.

Assessment should take place to focus on improving learning, while helping and motivating your learners towards the achievement of their qualification or learning outcomes. It should help your learners realise how they are progressing, what they need to do to improve and what support, if any, they may require. Successful achievement of an accredited qualification or units will lead to the issue of a certificate by an Awarding Organisation.

Assessment can happen before, during and at the end of a learning programme (initial, formative and summative). It should be an effective and regular process which incorporates informal and formal activities. You will be observing what your learners are doing, asking them questions and reviewing their progress probably every time you are in contact with them. You are therefore constantly making judgements about their development and discussing with them how they could improve. Informal and formal assessments will not only confirm learner success or otherwise, but will satisfy any organisational or regulatory requirements for standards to be maintained. If assessment did not take place, you would not know what skills, knowledge and/or attitudes had been learnt and applied competently. You also would not be able to develop further learning and assessment opportunities, or prove to an Awarding Organisation which criteria had been met.

Assessment should not be confused with evaluation: assessment is of the *learner*; evaluation is of the *programme*. Assessment is specific towards learners' achievements and how they can improve. Evaluation is a quality assurance monitoring tool. It includes feedback from your learners and others, for example employers, line managers and verifiers, to help you improve your own practice and the overall learner experience.

At level 4, in addition to the above, you should read relevant textbooks, articles and journals, and access appropriate websites, referring to them in your response. When writing, you should be analytical rather than descriptive and use a recognised academic style of writing.

For example, analysing and discussing a quote such as:

> *If assessment is to be seen as a valuable tool and respected by learners, colleagues and other stakeholders, then it must be seen to do what it purports to do, i.e. it must be effective.*
>
> (Wilson, 2008, p289)

You could obtain a copy of the syllabus or qualification handbook for your subject area to ensure that you understand the assessment requirements and that the criteria and required standards can be met and maintained.

Q43 What is the role of an assessor?

The role of an assessor is to follow the *assessment cycle* as shown in Figure 7.1 (Gravells, 2011), along with the requirements of the relevant Awarding Organisation (if applicable) and your own organisational requirements for assessing your subject. Your main role should be to ensure that your learners are on an appropriate programme and then inspire and motivate them to succeed. You should have a job description which outlines your role and responsibilities as an assessor; if not, there should be generic guidelines in the Awarding Organisation's syllabus or qualification handbook. You should also find out if you are required to be working towards or hold an appropriate assessor qualification.

Figure 7.1 Assessment Cycle (Gravells, 2011)

At level 4, in addition to the above, you should read relevant textbooks, articles and journals, and access appropriate websites, referring to them in your response. When writing, you should be analytical rather than descriptive and use a recognised academic style of writing.

For example, you could discuss what happens during each aspect of the assessment cycle and how it impacts upon your role as an assessor. You could compare it to theorists such as Kolb's (1984) Experiential Learning Cycle.

Q44 What is an assessment strategy and why have one?

An assessment strategy is a statement usually issued by the relevant Sector Skills Council, the body responsible for producing the qualification standards. The Awarding Organisation takes these standards and incorporates the assessment strategy into their syllabus or qualification handbook. The assessment strategy will state how the subject should be assessed, quality assured, and how subsequent results should be recorded. It should also state the experience, required professional development and qualifications that assessors should hold.

You should find out which your Sector Skills Council is and what their assessment strategy is for your subject. You should also locate your organisation's own assessment policy and ensure that you can follow the requirements. If your qualification is non-accredited, i.e. not offered by an Awarding Organisation, you could write your own assessment strategy if none exists within your organisation.

It is important to have an assessment strategy to ensure that a quality service is given to your learners and to maintain the reputation of your organisation and the qualification being assessed. For example, an inexperienced assessor might make a wrong decision which could lead to a learner submitting an appeal or being unsuccessful in achieving their qualification. The success of your organisation might be measured by funding agencies (if applicable), and penalties could be imposed where success is deemed to be below their standards.

At level 4, in addition to the above, you should read relevant textbooks, articles and journals, and access appropriate websites, referring to them in your response. When writing, you should be analytical rather than descriptive and use a recognised academic style of writing.

For example, you could compare and contrast different assessment strategies from various Sector Skills Councils. You could also review your organisation's assessment policy and recommend changes or improvements.

Q45 Identify the key concepts of assessment.

A concept is an idea, i.e. *what* is involved throughout the assessment process.

Identified key concepts could include:

- accountability;
- achievement;
- assessment strategies;
- benchmarking;
- evaluation;
- initial, formative or summative types;

- internally or externally devised methods (formal and informal);

- progression;

- transparency.

At level 4, in addition to the above, you should read relevant textbooks, articles and journals, and access appropriate websites, referring to them in your response. When writing, you should be analytical rather than descriptive and use a recognised academic style of writing.

For example, you could summarise the concepts in the bulleted list and make your responses specific to the subject you assess. Examples of the first three are given below.

You need to be *accountable* to your learners and your organisation to ensure you are carrying out your role as an assessor correctly. Your learners should always know why they are being assessed and what they have to do to meet the assessment criteria. You will also be accountable to the Awarding Organisation if you assess accredited programmes, or to employers if you are assessing bespoke programmes. You may be required to analyse *achievement* data and compare this to national or organisational targets. The funding your organisation receives will also be related to your learner achievements.

Following the *assessment strategy* for your subject will ensure you are carrying out your role correctly. You should state what the strategy is and what qualifications and experience you are expected to have.

Your response should refer to relevant legislation such as the Copyright, Designs and Patents Act (1988) and the Data Protection Act (2003). You will need to follow your organisation's codes of practice, policies and procedures relating to assessment, and you could refer to these within your response, for example in relation to appeals or plagiarism. You may need to attend team meetings and standardisation events to ensure you are assessing fairly and accurately.

Q46 Summarise the key principles of assessment.

Principles are rules and functions which are based upon the concepts, for example *how* the assessment process is put into practice.

Key principles of assessment include:

- CPD – maintaining currency of knowledge and competency to ensure assessment practice is up to date;

- equality and diversity – ensuring all assessment activities embrace equality, inclusivity and diversity and represent all aspects of society;

- ethics – ensuring the assessment process is honest and moral, and takes into account confidentiality and integrity;

- fairness – activities should be fit for purpose, and planning, decisions and feedback justifiable;

- health and safety – ensuring these are taken into account throughout the full assessment process, carrying out risk assessments as necessary;

- motivation – encouraging and supporting your learners to reach their maximum potential at an appropriate level;

- quality assurance – an integrated process ensuring assessment decisions meet the qualification standards, and assessors are carrying out their role correctly;

- record keeping – ensuring accurate records are maintained throughout the learning and assessment process, and communicating with others, for example an Awarding Organisation;

- SMART – ensuring all assessment activities are specific, measurable, achievable, realistic and timebound;

- standardisation – ensuring the assessment requirements are interpreted accurately and that all assessors are making comparable decisions;

- VACSR – ensuring all assessed work is valid, authentic, current, sufficient and reliable.

At level 4, in addition to the above, you should read relevant textbooks, articles and journals, and access appropriate websites, referring to them in your response. When writing, you should be analytical rather than descriptive and use a recognised academic style of writing.

For example, you could summarise details of each aspect in the previous bulleted list, for instance VACSR.

- **V**alid – the work is relevant to the assessment criteria.

- **A**uthentic – the work has been produced solely by the learner.

- **C**urrent – the work is still relevant at the time of assessment.

- **S**ufficient – the work covers all the assessment criteria.

- **R**eliable – the work is consistent across all learners, over time and at the required level.

Try to make your response specific to your specialist subject.

Theory focus

References and further information

Gravells A (2011) *Principles and Practice of Assessment in the Lifelong Learning Sector* (2nd edition). Exeter: Learning Matters

Kolb D (1984) *Experiential Learning: Experience as the Source for Learning and Development.* New Jersey: Prentice-Hall

Tummons J (2007) *Assessing Learning in the Lifelong Learning Sector* (2nd edition). Exeter: Learning Matters

Wilson L (2008) *Practical teaching: a guide to PTLLS and CTLLS.* London: Cengage Learning

Websites

Assessment guidance booklets – www.sflip.org.uk/assessment/assessmentguidance. aspx

Assessment Reform Group – www.assessment-reform-group.org/index.html

Chartered Institute of Educational Assessors – www.ciea.org.uk

Copyright, Designs and Patents Act (1988) – www.copyrightservice.co.uk/copyright/uk_law_summary

Data Protection Act (2003) – regulatorylaw.co.uk/Data_Protection_Act_2003.html

Plagiarism – www.plagiarism.org

Sector Skills Councils – www.sscalliance.org

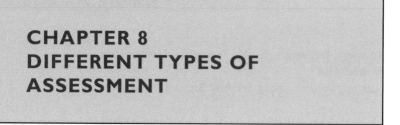

CHAPTER 8
DIFFERENT TYPES OF
ASSESSMENT

This chapter is in two parts. The first part, **Self-assessment activities**, contains questions and activities which relate to the second learning outcome of the CTLLS mandatory unit: *Principles and Practice of Assessment in the Lifelong Learning Sector – Understand and use different types of assessment.*

The assessment criteria for each level are shown in boxes and are followed by activities and questions for you to carry out. Ensure your responses are *specific to you*, the *subject* you will teach and the *context* and *environment* in which you will teach.

After completing the activities and questions, check your responses with the second part: **Guidance for evidencing competence**. This guidance is not intended to give you the answers to questions you may be asked in any formal assessments; however, it will help you focus your responses towards meeting the CTLLS requirements.

Self-assessment activities

Level 3 – 2.1 Explain and demonstrate how different types of assessment can be used effectively to meet the individual needs of learners

Level 4 – 2.1 Discuss and demonstrate how different types of assessment can be used effectively to meet the individual needs of learners

Q47 Explain the different types of assessment that you could use with your learners.

Q48 How will these effectively meet the needs of individual learners?

Q49 During one of your sessions, demonstrate the use of different types of assessment with your learners and reflect on how effective these were. Ensure your scheme of work and session/assessment plans show how the assessment types will be used.

Guidance for evidencing competence

Level 3 – 2.1 Explain and demonstrate how different types of assessment can be used effectively to meet the individual needs of learners

Level 4 – 2.1 Discuss and demonstrate how different types of assessment can be used effectively to meet the individual needs of learners

Q47 Explain the different types of assessment that you could use with your learners.

The types of assessment used at your organisation will vary depending upon the subject you are teaching and assessing. Your response should state the most commonly used ones which are usually initial (at the beginning), formative (ongoing) and summative (at the end).

Initial assessment is carried out prior to or at the beginning of a programme to identify your learner's starting point and level. Other initial assessments include learning styles tests, literacy, numeracy and ICT tests, and diagnostic tests to ascertain current knowledge and experience. Some types of diagnostic assessments can identify learners with dyslexia, dyspraxia, dysgraphia, dyscalculia, etc. Learner needs can also be ascertained through initial assessment.

Formative assessment is ongoing throughout a programme and can be used to assess attitudes, skills and/or knowledge in a progressive way, to build on topics learnt and plan future learning and assessments. It is usually informal, for example questions or discussions, whereas summative assessment is usually formal, for example an examination.

Summative assessment is carried out at the end of a qualification unit or programme to determine whether your learner has passed and what grade they have achieved (if applicable).

When planning which assessment type to use, you need to ensure it will be *valid* and *reliable*, and that you are being *fair* and *ethical* with all your decisions.

- Valid – the assessment type is appropriate to the subject/qualification being assessed.

- Reliable – if the assessment is carried out again with similar learners, similar results will be achieved.

- Fair – the assessment type is appropriate to all your learners at the required level, is inclusive, i.e. available to all, and differentiates for any particular needs.

- Ethical – the assessment takes into account confidentiality, integrity, safety and security.

At level 4, in addition to the above, you should read relevant textbooks, articles and journals, and access appropriate websites, referring to them in your response. When writing, you should be analytical rather than descriptive and use a recognised academic style of writing.

You could discuss other types of assessment such as ipsative, norm referencing and criterion referencing.

Ipsative is a process of self-assessment. Learners match their own achievements against a set of standards, or keep a reflective journal of their learning so far.

Norm referencing compares the results of learner achievements to each other, for example by setting a pass mark to enable a certain percentage of a group to achieve or not.

Criterion referencing enables learners to achieve based upon their own merit, as their achievements are not compared to each other. All learners therefore have equality of opportunity. If grades are allocated, for example a distinction, credit or pass, there will be specific criteria which must have been met for each. These criteria will either be supplied by the Awarding Organisation, or you may need to produce them yourself.

You could produce a case study regarding the different types of assessment you have used with your learners, how effective they were, what changes you would make and why.

Q48 How will these effectively meet the needs of individual learners?

You will need to state which assessment types you use and how they can effectively meet the needs of your individual learners. The following information is based on those mentioned in the previous question; however, you will need to make your responses specific to your own particular learners and subject specialism.

- Initial assessment – ascertaining a learner's prior knowledge and experience will identify a relevant starting point for assessment opportunities to alleviate duplication. It will also identify their learning style so you are able to match an appropriate assessment method. Knowing some details about a learner's needs will help improve their experience, for example if they are working shifts and cannot be assessed at particular times, or if they require training to use a computer.

- Formative assessment – carrying out ongoing assessment throughout a learner's programme will ascertain how they are progressing at a given point. If they are not doing so well, further training can be arranged and/or alternative assessments planned. It is best to find out during the programme rather than at the end when little can be done to help them. Formative assessments can include oral questions, a quiz, a practical demonstration or a worksheet.

- Summative assessment – assessment at the end of a qualification unit or programme will determine what the learner has achieved. Some learners cope well under pressure, for example taking an examination. However, others may get anxious and although are very capable otherwise, may not pass due to being nervous. Carrying out a mock assessment prior to the actual assessment could help some learners prepare themselves.

At level 4, in addition to the above, you should read relevant textbooks, articles and journals, and access appropriate websites, referring to them in your response. When writing, you should be analytical rather than descriptive and use a recognised academic style of writing.

For example, you could elaborate on other types of assessment such as ipsative, norm referencing and criterion referencing.

- Ipsative – some learners are very good at assessing their own progress; however, they do need to be honest with responses. Completing checklists or writing a reflective journal can help learners identify their achievements towards the qualification. Ipsative assessments are good for more mature or higher level learners who can analyse what they have achieved so far.

- Norm referencing – this will pitch learners against each other and can increase competition to achieve. For example, if the pass mark is 80 per cent then only some learners will achieve depending upon the criteria which have been set. This could encourage some learners to work harder or could disadvantage others.

- Criterion referencing – this enables learners to be assessed towards particular outcomes of a qualification. They are not pitched against others and can achieve when they are ready. Criterion referencing assessment is good for learners to demonstrate practical skills, for example in their place of work.

You could produce a case study analysing how different types of assessment meet the individual needs of your learners. For instance, you might use larger print, allow additional time, adapt equipment and resources or modify the assessment activities. Any changes should always be approved by your Awarding Organisation and not give any learner an unfair advantage in any way.

Q49 During one of your sessions, demonstrate the use of different types of assessment with your learners and reflect how effective these were. Ensure your scheme of work and session/ assessment plans show how the assessment types will be used.

This is a practical task enabling you to use different types of assessment with your learners. You are required to deliver at least 30 teaching practice hours throughout your time working towards the CTLLS qualification. You will be observed by your assessor for some of this time and they will need to see that you have used different types of assessment. They will give you verbal and written feedback and you should take this into account when reflecting on how effective the assessment types were. You could write a self-evaluation or reflective learning journal to discuss how the assessment types met the individual needs of your learners during a particular session. Evidence you could provide includes your scheme of work and session plans showing how the assessment types will be used, along with the actual assessment activities. You could assess learners in their place of work and provide assessment plans, checklists and feedback records. You might also deliver a short micro-teach session to your peers to demonstrate your knowledge of different types of assessment.

At level 4, in addition to the above, you should read relevant textbooks, articles and journals, and access appropriate websites, referring to them in your response. When writing, you should be analytical rather than descriptive and use a recognised academic style of writing.

For example, you could discuss Schön (1991) who suggests two methods of reflection:

● in action;

● on action.

Reflection *in action* happens at the time of the incident, is often unconscious and allows immediate changes to take place. Reflection *on action* takes place after the incident and is a more conscious process. This allows you time to think about the incident, consider a different approach, or to talk to others about it before making changes. You could give an example of each within your ongoing reflective learning journal where you have made a change *in action* or *on action*.

Theory focus

References and further information

Gravells A (2011) *Principles and Practice of Assessment in the Lifelong Learning Sector* (2nd edition). Exeter: Learning Matters

Reece I and Walker S (2007) *Teaching training and learning: a practical guide* (6th edition). Tyne and Wear: Business Education Publishers Ltd

Roffey-Barentsen J and Malthouse R (2009) *Reflective Practice in the Lifelong Learning Sector.* Exeter: Learning Matters

Schön D (1991) *The Reflective Practitioner: How professionals think in action.* Farnham: Ashgate Publishing Ltd

Tummons J (2007) *Assessing Learning in the Lifelong Learning Sector* (2nd edition). Exeter: Learning Matters

Wallace S (2007) *Achieving QTLS: Teaching, Tutoring and Training in the Lifelong Learning Sector* (3rd edition). Exeter: Learning Matters

Websites

Initial Assessment Tools – www.toolslibrary.co.uk

Learning Styles – www.vark-learn.com

CHAPTER 9
THE STRENGTHS AND LIMITATIONS OF A RANGE OF ASSESSMENT METHODS

This chapter is in two parts. The first part, *Self-assessment activities*, contains questions and activities which relate to the third learning outcome of the CTLLS mandatory unit: *Principles and Practice of Assessment in the Lifelong Learning Sector – Understand the strengths and limitations of a range of assessment methods, including, as appropriate, those which exploit new and emerging technologies.*

The assessment criteria for each level are shown in boxes and are followed by activities and questions for you to carry out. Ensure your responses are *specific to you*, the *subject* you will teach and the *context* and *environment* in which you will teach.

After completing the activities and questions, check your responses with the second part: *Guidance for evidencing competence*. This guidance is not intended to give you the answers to questions you may be asked in any formal assessments; however, it will help you focus your responses towards meeting the CTLLS requirements.

Self-assessment activities

> Level 3 – 3.1 Identify the strengths and limitations of a range of assessment methods with reference to the needs of particular learners and key concepts and principles of assessment
>
> Level 4 – 3.1 Evaluate a range of assessment methods with reference to the needs of particular learners and key concepts and principles of assessment

Q50 Identify a range of assessment methods that can be used to assess your learners. When responding, consider the key concepts and principles of assessment referred to in Chapter 7.

Q51 What are the strengths and limitations of your identified assessment methods?

Q52 How can you use new and emerging technologies within the assessment process?

Q53 How can you ensure the assessment methods you use address the needs of particular learners?

Level 3 – 3.2 Use a range of assessment methods appropriately to ensure that learners produce assessment evidence that is valid, reliable, sufficient, authentic and current

Level 4 – 3.2 Use a range of assessment methods appropriately to ensure that learners produce assessment evidence that is valid, reliable, sufficient, authentic and current

Q54 Use a range of assessment methods with your learners, ensuring the evidence you assess is valid, reliable, sufficient, authentic and current.

Level 3 – 3.3 Explain how the use of peer and self-assessment can be used to promote learner involvement and personal responsibility in the assessment of their learning

Level 4 – 3.3 Justify the use of peer and self-assessment to promote learner involvement and personal responsibility in the assessment of their learning

Q55 Explain what the terms peer and self-assessment mean.

Q56 Explain how peer and self-assessment can be used to promote learner involvement and personal responsibility.

Guidance for evidencing competence

Level 3 – 3.1 Identify the strengths and limitations of a range of assessment methods with reference to the needs of particular learners and key concepts and principles of assessment

Level 4 – 3.1 Evaluate a range of assessment methods with reference to the needs of particular learners and key concepts and principles of assessment

Q50 Identify a range of assessment methods that can be used to assess your learners. When responding, consider the key concepts and principles of assessment referred to in Chapter 7.

To ensure variety within the assessment process and maximise your learners' opportunities to achieve, it is best to use a range of assessment methods.

Some of the methods you may have identified include:

- assignments;
- case studies;
- examinations;
- observations;
- peer assessments;
- professional discussions;
- projects;
- puzzles and quizzes;
- questions – written and oral;
- RPL;
- reflective learning journals;
- self-assessments;
- simulations;
- tests;
- witness statements.

When responding, you should explain how your methods address the key concepts of:

- accountability;

- achievement;

- assessment strategies;

- benchmarking;

- evaluation;

- initial, formative or summative types;

- internally or externally devised methods (formal and informal);

- progression;

- transparency.

For example, using an assignment with your learners will ensure *accountability* to the Awarding Organisation by ensuring it meets the assessment criteria. Ensuring your learners are capable of *achieving* their chosen programme or qualification will satisfy internal and external requirements. The *assessment strategy* should be followed, i.e. all assessors should be appropriately qualified and/or experienced at the subject being assessed. *Benchmarking* can be used to set targets for individuals or groups. Self-*evaluation* and learner *evaluation* should take place to gain feedback in order to improve the assessment process. The assessment types used, i.e. *initial, formative or summative* should be relevant to the *formal* and *informal* methods used to assess your subject. All learners should be aware of how they can *progress* further, perhaps with an action plan for development or a revised assessment plan. *Transparency* will be achieved by everyone clearly understanding what is expected and by keeping accurate records which should be subject to internal quality assurance.

At level 4, in addition to the above, you should read relevant textbooks, articles and journals, and access appropriate websites, referring to them in your response. When writing, you should be analytical rather than descriptive and use a recognised academic style of writing.

For example, you could evaluate your identified assessment methods stating how effective they have been for your learners. You should relate your response to the principles of assessment referred to in Chapter 7, question 46.

Q51 What are the strengths and limitations of your identified assessment methods?

Table 9.1 gives the strengths and limitations of some of the methods identified in question 50. A full table appears in the book *Principles and Practice of Assessment in the Lifelong Learning Sector* (Gravells, 2011).

Table 9.1 Strengths and limitations of a range of assessment methods

Method	Strengths	Limitations
Assignments	Can challenge a learner's potential Consolidates learning Several aspects of a qualification can be assessed Some assignments are set by the Awarding Organisation which will give clear marking criteria	Must ensure all aspects of the syllabus have been taught beforehand Can be time consuming to prepare and assess Must be individually assessed and written feedback given Assessor might be biased when marking
Learning journals	Develops self-assessment skills Relates theory to practice Helps assess language and literacy Useful for higher level qualifications	Should be specific to the learning taking place and be analytical rather than descriptive Content needs to remain confidential Can be time consuming and/or difficult to read
Observations	Enables skills to be seen in action Learners can make a mistake (if it is safe to do so) enabling them to realise what they have done wrong Can assess several aspects of a qualification at the same time (holistic assessment)	Timing must be arranged to suit each learner Communication needs to take place with others (if at a learner's workplace) No permanent record unless visually recorded or notes taken Questions must be asked to confirm understanding Assessor might not be objective
Professional discussions	Useful to support observations to check knowledge Learners can describe how they carry out various activities	A record must be kept of the discussion, e.g. audio/digital/visual along with notes Needs careful planning as it is a discussion not a question and answer session Learners need time to prepare Assessor needs to be experienced at questioning and listening skills
Questions (written and oral)	Can be multiple choice, short answer or long essay style Can challenge and promote a learner's potential A question bank can be devised to randomly choose from for different learners Can test critical arguments or thinking and reasoning skills Oral questions suit some learners more than others, e.g. a dyslexic learner might prefer to talk through their responses	Closed questions only give a yes or no response which does not demonstrate knowledge Questions must be written carefully, i.e. be unambiguous, and can be time consuming to prepare If the same questions are used with other learners, they could share their answers Written responses might be the work of others, i.e. copied or plagiarised Expected responses or grading criteria need to be produced beforehand to ensure consistency and validity of judgements May need to rephrase some questions if learners are struggling with an answer

At level 4, in addition to the above, you should read relevant textbooks, articles and journals, and access appropriate websites, referring to them in your response. When writing, you should be analytical rather than descriptive and use a recognised academic style of writing.

For example, you could evaluate how assessment activities take into account the following:

- availability of resources;
- differentiation;
- equality and diversity;
- health and safety;
- inclusivity;
- learner needs;
- level of learning;
- the environment.

Records must always be maintained to prove your learners' achievements. Your response could state the types of records you use, for example assessment plans, tutorial reviews, observation reports and feedback records, along with the reasons why. You could also make recommendations regarding changes you would make to activities or documentation, along with the reasons why.

Q52 How can you use new and emerging technologies within the assessment process?

Technology is constantly evolving and new resources are frequently becoming available. It is crucial to keep up to date with new developments and try and incorporate these within the assessment process. It is not only about you using technology to help assess your learners, but also about your learners using it to complete their assessment activities. Encouraging your learners to use technology will help increase their skills in this area.

Your response should state that technology can be combined with traditional methods of assessments, for example learners can complete a written assignment by word-processing their response and submitting it by e-mail or uploading it to a secure website. You can then give informal feedback when you next see your learner and formal feedback via the website. Combining methods also promotes differentiation and inclusivity, for example learners could access assessment materials and feedback via a VLE outside the normal learning environment to support their learning.

New and emerging technologies include using:

- blogs, chat rooms and online discussion forums to help learners communicate with each other;

- cameras and mobile phones for taking pictures;

- computer facilities for learners to word-process their assignments and save documents and pictures;

- digital media for visual/audio recording and playback;

- electronic portfolios enabling learners to store their work;

- e-mail for electronic submission of assessments, communication and informal feedback on progress;

- interactive whiteboards for learners to use and display their work;

- internet access for research to support assignments;

- mobile phones for taking pictures, video and audio clips and communicating;

- networked systems to allow access to programs and documents from any computer linked to the system;

- online and on-demand tests which can give instant results, for example diagnostic and multiple choice tests;

- online discussion forums which allow asynchronous (taking place at different times) and synchronous (taking place at the same time) discussions;

- presentation software and equipment for learners to give presentations;

- scanners for copying and transferring documents to a computer;

- web cameras or video conferencing if you cannot be in the same place as your learners and you need to observe a task;

- VLEs to upload supporting materials and assessment activities.

At level 4, in addition to the above, you should read relevant textbooks, articles and journals, and access appropriate websites, referring to them in your response. When writing, you should be analytical rather than descriptive and use a recognised academic style of writing.

You could produce a case study evaluating a particular type of technology you have used with your learners, stating the advantages and limitations. These could include:

- advantages:
  - auditable and reliable;
  - accessible and inclusive;

- addresses sustainability, i.e. no need for paper copies;
- efficient use of time and cost effective;
- immediate results can be obtained from online tests;
- learners can access resources and materials at a time and place to suit;
- tests can be on demand.

- limitations:
  - can lead to plagiarism of text via the internet;
  - cannot be used during power cuts;
  - finance required to purchase new technology and computers;
  - might create barriers if learners cannot access or use technology;
  - not enough resources for all learners to use at the same time;
  - some learners might be afraid of using new technology;
  - time consuming to initially set up.

Try and make your response specific to the technology you are using with your learners.

Q53 How can you ensure the assessment methods you use address the needs of particular learners?

To ensure the assessment methods used address the needs of particular learners you should always include all learners within the assessment process, for example during a group activity, and differentiate for any particular needs. Differentiation can be achieved by using alternative assessment activities, for example to meet different levels of learning. However, you will need to know the needs of your learners to be able to address them. Initial assessment, tutorials and reviews should help you gain this information.

Your response could include examples of meeting learner needs, including the following.

- A disability – learners could be assessed in a more comfortable environment where appropriate access and support systems are available. Learners could be given extra time to complete the assessment tasks, or to take medication privately, dates for assessment could be rearranged to fit around doctor or hospital appointments.

- A hearing impairment – an induction loop could be used where all or part of an assessment is presented orally. Instructions and questions could be conveyed using sign language.

- A visual impairment – using large print or Braille, using specialist computer software if available, asking questions verbally and making an audio recording of your learner's responses.

- Dyslexia – allowing additional time if necessary and/or the use of a word processor to type responses. Presenting written questions in a more simplified format, for example bullet points and using pastel coloured paper and printing in a different font. Asking questions verbally and making an audio or visual recording of your learner's responses.

- English as a second or other language – using an interpreter, if possible try and arrange assessments in your learner's first language, for example Welsh. Many Awarding Organisations can translate assessment materials if requested.

- Learner support – generic support relating to the learning and assessment experience, for example advice, counselling, crèche, transport, etc.

- Learning support – specific support relating to the achievement of the qualification, the Functional Skills of English, maths and ICT, help with study and research skills, support with academic writing and referencing, etc.

- Learning styles – adapting the assessment activities to suit the styles of the learners.

- Levels of learning – using different activities, for example quizzes for lower level learners, written questions for higher levels.

- Varying work patterns – trying to be flexible and arranging the assessment at a time and place to suit both learner and assessor.

If you need to adapt any assessment activities for an accredited qualification, you will need to check with the Awarding Organisation first. You may need to liaise with others in your organisation regarding any specific needs that you are not able to help with, for example using an interpreter or lip reader.

At level 4, in addition to the above, you should read relevant textbooks, articles and journals, and access appropriate websites, referring to them in your response. When writing, you should be analytical rather than descriptive and use a recognised academic style of writing.

For example, you could refer to the codes of practice, policies and procedures within your organisation regarding learner support. You could also refer to legislation such as the Disability Discrimination Act (2005) and how this has impacted upon your role as an assessor.

You could produce a case study of how you have addressed the needs of particular learners with subject specific assessments, ensuring you maintain confidentially of names.

> Level 3 – 3.2 Use a range of assessment methods appropriately to ensure that learners produce assessment evidence that is valid, reliable, sufficient, authentic and current
>
> Level 4 – 3.2 Use a range of assessment methods appropriately to ensure that learners produce assessment evidence that is valid, reliable, sufficient, authentic and current

Q54 Use a range of assessment methods with your learners, ensuring the evidence you assess is valid, reliable, sufficient, authentic and current.

This is a practical task which enables you to use a range of assessment methods with your learners. You could use those mentioned in your response to question 50 and then evaluate whether the evidence was valid, reliable, sufficient, authentic and current. Evidence you could provide includes assessment plans you have prepared with your learners along with the actual assessment activities, for example an assignment, and evidence of your decisions and the feedback given. You might also be observed by your assessor who should provide you with an observation checklist and verbal and/or written feedback.

At level 4, in addition to the above, you should read relevant textbooks, articles and journals, and access appropriate websites, referring to them in your response. When writing, you should be analytical rather than descriptive and use a recognised academic style of writing.

For example, you could evaluate the assessment methods you have used, stating what went well, what you would improve, what you would change for next time and why.

> Level 3 – 3.3 Explain how the use of peer and self-assessment can be used to promote learner involvement and personal responsibility in the assessment of their learning
>
> Level 4 – 3.3 Justify the use of peer and self-assessment to promote learner involvement and personal responsibility in the assessment of their learning

Q55 Explain what the terms peer and self-assessment mean.

Peer assessment involves a learner or colleague assessing another learner's or colleague's progress. Self-assessment involves a learner assessing their own progress. Both methods encourage learners to make decisions about what has been learnt so far, and to reflect on aspects for further development. Your learners will need to fully understand the assessment criteria, and be analytical and objective with their judgements.

You could state the advantages and limitations of each, for example:

- peer assessment advantages:
  - can reduce the amount of teacher assessment;
  - increases attention for activities such as peer presentations if feedback has to be given;
  - learners are more focussed upon the assessment criteria;
  - learners may accept comments from peers more readily than those from the assessor;
  - promotes learner and peer interaction and involvement.
- peer assessment limitations:
  - all peers should be involved so planning needs to take place as to who will give feedback to whom;
  - appropriate conditions and environment are needed;
  - assessor needs to confirm each learner's progress and achievements as it might be different from their peer's judgement;
  - everyone needs to understand the assessment criteria;
  - learners might be subjective and friendly rather than objective with their decisions;
  - needs to be carefully managed to avoid personality conflicts and unjustified comments;
  - should be supported with other assessment methods;
  - some peers may be anxious, nervous or lack confidence to give feedback.
- self-assessment advantages:
  - encourages learners to check their own progress;
  - encourages reflection;
  - mistakes can be seen as opportunities;
  - promotes learner involvement and personal responsibility.
- self-assessment limitations:
  - assessor needs to discuss and confirm progress and achievement;
  - difficult to be objective when making a decision;
  - learners may feel they have achieved more than they actually have;
  - learners must fully understand the assessment criteria;
  - learners need to be specific about what they have achieved and what they need to do to fill in any gaps;
  - some learners may lack confidence in their ability to make decisions about their own progress.

At level 4, in addition to the above, you should read relevant textbooks, articles and journals, and access appropriate websites, referring to them in your response. When writing, you should be analytical rather than descriptive and use a recognised academic style of writing.

For example, you could critically analyse Boud (1995), the theorist who suggested that learning and development will not occur without self-assessment and reflection. You could research other relevant theorists and compare and contrast your findings.

Q56 Explain how peer and self-assessment can be used to promote learner involvement and personal responsibility.

Peer and self-assessment can promote learner involvement and personal responsibility by encouraging ownership of the learning process. All learners should be fully aware of the requirements of the qualification and therefore ensure their work is focussed upon the assessment criteria. Throughout the process learners can develop skills such as communication, listening, observing and questioning.

The peer and self-assessment process provides opportunities for feedback and discussion regarding progress and areas for development. A template or pro-forma could be used to help standardise responses and decisions, to ensure learners keep to the assessment criteria. Peer feedback could be written rather than verbal and therefore be anonymous. This would encourage objective opinions as learners will not feel they are betraying their friends. Ground rules should be established to ensure the process is valid and fair.

Examples of peer and self-assessment activities include:

● a written statement of how they could improve their own or peers' work;

● assessing each other's work anonymously and giving written or verbal feedback;

● completing templates or pro-formas;

● giving grades and/or written or verbal feedback regarding own or peer presentations;

● group discussions before collectively agreeing a grade and giving feedback perhaps for a presentation;

● proposing a grade for their own or peers' work;

● suggesting improvements to their own or peers' work.

At level 4, in addition to the above, you should read relevant textbooks, articles and journals, and access appropriate websites, referring to them in your response. When writing, you should be analytical rather than descriptive and use a recognised academic style of writing.

For example, you could justify how peer and self-assessment can promote learner involvement and personal responsibility. This could be a justification of how and why you used both peer and self-assessment within your sessions with your own learners. You might be required to use peer assessment with others taking the CTLLS qualification, perhaps as part of a micro-teach session. You could therefore justify your reasons for the feedback you gave. Conversely you might need to assess your own progress towards an aspect of the CTLLS qualification, for example how you felt your teaching practice session went. You would need to justify how you met the CTLLS assessment criteria and what you would do differently next time.

Theory focus

References and further information

Boud D (1995) *Enhancing learning through self-assessment.* London: Kogan Page

Gravells A (2011) *Principles and Practice of Assessment in the Lifelong Learning Sector* (2nd edition). Exeter: Learning Matters

Gravells A and Simpson S (2009) *Equality and Diversity in the Lifelong Learning Sector.* Exeter: Learning Matters

Hill C (2008) *Teaching with e-learning in the Lifelong Learning Sector* (2nd edition). Exeter: Learning Matters

QCA (2007) *Regulatory principles for e-assessment.* London: Qualifications and Curriculum Authority

Tummons T (2007) *Assessing Learning in the Lifelong Learning Sector.* Exeter: Learning Matters

Websites

Assessment methods – www.brookes.ac.uk/services/ocsd/2_learntch/methods.html

Disability Discrimination Act – www.opsi.gov.uk/acts/acts2005/ukpga_20050013_en_1

Efutures (e-assessment regulators) – www.e-assessment.org.uk

Equality and Diversity Forum – www.edf.org.uk

Open University inclusive practice – www.open.ac.uk/inclusiveteaching/pages/inclusive-teaching/index.php

Peer and self-assessment – www.nclrc.org/essentials/assessing/peereval.htm

Support for adult learners – www.direct.gov.uk/adultlearning

This chapter is in two parts. The first part, *Self-assessment activities*, contains questions and activities which relate to the fourth learning outcome of the CTLLS mandatory unit: *Principles and Practice of Assessment in the Lifelong Learning Sector – Understand the role of feedback and questioning in the assessment of learning.*

The assessment criteria for each level are shown in boxes and are followed by activities and questions for you to carry out. Ensure your responses are *specific to you*, the *subject* you will teach and the *context* and *environment* in which you will teach.

After completing the activities and questions, check your responses with the second part: *Guidance for evidencing competence*. This guidance is not intended to give you the answers to questions you may be asked in any formal assessments; however, it will help you focus your responses towards meeting the CTLLS requirements.

Self-assessment activities

> Level 3 – 4.1 Explain how feedback and questioning contributes to the assessment process
>
> Level 4 – 4.1 Analyse how feedback and questioning contributes to the assessment process

Q57 What is feedback and how can it effectively be given to learners?

Q58 Analyse how feedback and questioning can contribute to the assessment process.

> Level 3 – 4.2 Use feedback and questioning effectively in the assessment of learning
>
> Level 4 – 4.2 Use feedback and questioning effectively in the assessment of learning

Q59 Use feedback and questioning effectively in the assessment of learning. Evaluate how effective the process was.

Guidance for evidencing competence

Level 3 – 4.1 Explain how feedback and questioning contributes to the assessment process

Level 4 – 4.1 Analyse how feedback and questioning contributes to the assessment process

Q57 What is feedback and how can it effectively be given to learners?

Feedback is information you give to your learners to let them know what they have achieved at a given point, and how they can develop further. All learners need to know how they are progressing and what they have achieved; feedback should help reassure, boost confidence, encourage and motivate. Your response should state that feedback can be given formally, i.e. in writing, or informally, i.e. verbally, and should be given at a level which is appropriate for each learner. Feedback can be direct, i.e. to an individual, or indirect, i.e. to a group. It should be more thorough than just a quick comment and should include specific facts which relate to progress, success or otherwise. Records of decisions made regarding assessment and the feedback given should always be maintained. This is not only to satisfy regulatory bodies but to keep track of individual achievements.

Feedback can be formative and summative. Formative feedback is ongoing and includes praise and encouragement. Summative feedback is a decision as to your learner's achievement towards specific criteria, along with details about how they could develop further, if applicable.

If possible, feedback should be a two-way process, allowing a discussion and questioning to take place to clarify any points. If you are giving verbal feedback be aware of your body language, facial expressions and tone of voice. Do not use confrontational words or phrases likely to cause offence such as racist or stereotypical remarks. Take into account any non-verbal signals from your learners; you may need to adapt your feedback if you see they are becoming uncomfortable.

Feedback should never just be an evaluative statement like *well done*, or *that's great you've passed*. This doesn't tell your learner what was done well, or what was great about it. Your learner will be pleased to know they have passed; however, they won't have anything to build upon for the future. Descriptive feedback lets you describe what your learner has done, how they have achieved it and what they can do to progress further. It enables you to provide opportunities for your learner to make any adjustments or improvements to reach a particular standard.

Most people need encouragement, to be told when they are doing something well and why. When giving feedback it can really help your learner to hear first what they have done well followed by what they need to improve, and then to end on a positive note to keep them motivated. This is known as the *praise sandwich*. Often, the word *but* is used to link these points; replacing this with the word *however* is much easier for your learner to hear. Negative feedback, if given skillfully, can also help your learners' progress.

Using your learner's name makes the feedback more personal, and making the feedback specific enables your learner to appreciate what they need to do to improve. You will need to find out from your organisation how they require you to give feedback, for example writing in the first, second or third person. You also need to know whether it should be given verbally and/or in writing, and formally or informally, how much detail should be given, what forms must be completed and what records must be maintained.

The advantages of giving feedback are that it:

- confirms achievement, success or otherwise;

- creates opportunities for clarification and discussion;

- emphasises progress rather than failure;

- helps improve confidence and motivation;

- identifies further learning opportunities or any action required.

You could ask for feedback from your learners as to how they felt about the assessment process. This will help you improve your own skills and gain information which may be required by your Awarding Organisation.

At level 4, in addition to the above, you should read relevant textbooks, articles and journals, and access appropriate websites, referring to them in your response. When writing, you should be analytical rather than descriptive and use a recognised academic style of writing.

For example, you could analyse how you give feedback to your learners and how they react to receiving it by referring to theorists such as Skinner (1968). He argued that learners need to make regular *active responses*. These responses need immediate feedback with differential follow-ups, depending upon whether or not they were correct. Without immediate feedback, especially when the response is wrong, your learner will carry on making the same mistake thinking they are right. They will then have to unlearn their response. Time can be wasted by learners unlearning their wrong responses instead of learning new behaviours. You could also refer to Maslow's (1954) Hierarchy of Needs. He believed that recognition of learner achievement and positive feedback helps the need for recognition and self-actualisation.

Q58 Analyse how feedback and questioning can contribute to the assessment process.

Feedback and questioning can contribute to the assessment process by enabling your learners to be included in the course of their development and achievement. It gives them the opportunity to discuss and clarify aspects of their progress rather than just being told. The process also creates opportunities for your learners to ask questions and to provide feedback on their own learning.

The timing of feedback is important; it should be as soon as possible after the assessment decision has been made, while information is still fresh. If feedback is verbal, you should allow enough time for a discussion to take place, and the environment should be suitable, i.e. distractions should be minimised. Using your learner's name when talking to them helps make the feedback more personal. If feedback is written, for example on an assignment, this should be given in person if possible to allow for any clarification to take place.

Questioning can be used formally and informally as part of the feedback process to check your learner understands what you are saying. Try not to ask more than one question in a sentence as your learner will probably only respond to the last part of the sentence. Rephrase any questions if you feel your learner is struggling; perhaps the level of language or jargon you are using is causing confusion.

Your response should analyse appropriate questioning skills which ensure the process of feedback is effective for your learners.

Questioning skills include:

- using open questions (usually beginning with *who, what, when, where, why* and *how*);
- using closed questions (only requiring a *yes* or *no* answer);
- clarifying (for example, *Can you go over that again?*);
- probing (for example, *Why was that?*);
- prompting (for example, *What about …?*).

Having good listening skills will help you engage your learners in a conversation by hearing what they are saying and responding to any questions or concerns. Giving your learners time to talk will encourage them to inform you of things they might not otherwise have said, for example if something has had an effect upon their progress. Listening for key words will help you focus upon what is being said, for example *I struggled with the last part of the assignment*. The key word is *struggled* and you could therefore ask a question such as, *What made you struggle?* This would allow a conversation to then take place, giving you the opportunity to help and motivate your learner.

At level 4, in addition to the above, you should read relevant textbooks, articles and journals, and access appropriate websites, referring to them in your response. When writing, you should be analytical rather than descriptive and use a recognised academic style of writing.

You could refer to research such as that by Hattie and Timperley (2007) regarding the power and effectiveness of feedback. Regarding research they have undertaken, they state: *This evidence shows that although feedback is among the major influences, the type of feedback and the way it is given can be differentially effective* (p81). After reading this research, you could compare and contrast it to the type of feedback you give and the impact it has upon your learners.

> Level 3 – 4.2 Use feedback and questioning effectively in the assessment of learning
>
> Level 4 – 4.2 Use feedback and questioning effectively in the assessment of learning

Q59 Use feedback and questioning effectively in the assessment of learning. Evaluate how effective the process was.

This is a practical task which enables you to use feedback and questioning in the assessment of learning. Evidence you could provide includes your written assessment feedback records, tutorial review records, observation checklists from your assessor, witness and learner testimonies, and an audio or visual recording of the process.

After giving feedback, you should evaluate how effective the process was, for example in your reflective learning journals. You might realise that you did not allow enough time for your learner to ask questions, or you kept interrupting them. It is important to remain factual about what you have assessed and to be objective with your judgements. You should never compromise and pass a learner just because you like them, feel they have worked hard or are under pressure to achieve targets. You could therefore set yourself an action plan to improve your own feedback and questioning skills for the future.

At level 4, in addition to the above, you should read relevant textbooks, articles and journals, and access appropriate websites, referring to them in your response. When writing, you should be analytical rather than descriptive and use a recognised academic style of writing.

For example, you could produce a case study of how you used feedback and questioning with a particular learner, how this helped or hindered their development and the difference it made.

Theory focus

References and further information

Gravells A (2011) *Principles and Practice of Assessment in the Lifelong Learning Sector* (2nd edition). Exeter: Learning Matters

Hattie J and Timperley H (2007) The Power of Feedback. *Review of Educational Research*, 77(1): 81–112

Maslow A (1954) *Motivation and Personality* New York: Harper

Skinner B (1968) *The Technology of Teaching.* New York: Appleton, Century & Crofts

Tummons T (2007) *Assessing Learning in the Lifelong Learning Sector.* Exeter: Learning Matters

Websites

Assessment guidance booklets – www.sflip.org.uk/assessment/assessmentguidance.aspx

Assessment methods in higher education – www.brookes.ac.uk/services/ocsd/2_learntch/methods.html

CHAPTER 11
HOW TO MONITOR, ASSESS, RECORD AND REPORT LEARNER PROGRESS AND ACHIEVEMENT

This chapter is in two parts. The first part, *Self-assessment activities*, contains questions and activities which relate to the fifth learning outcome of the CTLLS mandatory unit: *Principles and Practice of Assessment in the Lifelong Learning Sector – Understand how to monitor, assess, record and report learner progress and achievement to meet the requirements of the learning programme and the organisation.*

The assessment criteria for each level are shown in boxes and are followed by activities and questions for you to carry out. Ensure your responses are *specific to you*, the *subject* you will teach and the *context* and *environment* in which you will teach.

After completing the activities and questions, check your responses with the second part: **Guidance for evidencing competence**. This guidance is not intended to give you the answers to questions you may be asked in any formal assessments; however, it will help you focus your responses towards meeting the CTLLS requirements.

Self-assessment activities

Level 3 – 5.1 Specify the assessment requirements and related procedures of a particular learning programme

Level 4 – 5.1 Review the assessment requirements and related procedures of a particular learning programme

Q60 What is the title or subject of the learning programme you will assess? Is it externally accredited? If so, which is your Awarding Organisation?

Q61 Review the requirements and related procedures you must follow to ensure that assessment is effective.

Level 3 – 5.2 Conduct and record assessments which meet the requirements of the learning programme and the organisation including, where appropriate, the requirements of external bodies

Level 4 – 5.2 Conduct and record assessments which meet the requirements of the learning programme and the organisation including, where appropriate, the requirements of external bodies

Q62 Conduct an assessment activity with your learners which meets the requirements of the learning programme.

Q63 What would influence your judgement and decision as to whether the activity has met the requirements of the programme, your organisation and external bodies?

Q64 What documentation is used during the assessment process with your learners and why?

Level 3 – 5.3 Communicate relevant assessment information to those with a legitimate interest in learner achievement

Level 4 – 5.3 Communicate relevant assessment information to those with a legitimate interest in learner achievement

Q65 Who has a legitimate interest in your learners' achievement besides yourself?

Q66 How do you communicate relevant assessment information to them?

Guidance for evidencing competence

Level 3 – 5.1 Specify the assessment requirements and related procedures of a particular learning programme

Level 4 – 5.1 Review the assessment requirements and related procedures of a particular learning programme

Q60 What is the title or subject of the learning programme you will assess? Is it externally accredited? If so, which is your Awarding Organisation?

When responding to this question you should find out the exact title or subject of the programme and qualification you will be assessing and specify what this is. Often, the title or subject of the programme is different to the actual qualification. For example, a programme called *Computing for Beginners* might lead to a qualification called *Level 1 Award in Information and Communication Technology* and be accredited by various Awarding Organisations such as City & Guilds or Edexcel. You need to find out who accredits the qualification you will be assessing and ensure you have an up-to-date copy of their syllabus or qualification handbook.

At level 4, in addition to the above, you should read relevant textbooks, articles and journals, and access appropriate websites, referring to them in your response. When writing, you should be analytical rather than descriptive and use a recognised academic style of writing.

For example, you could analyse which learning programmes in your organisation are given a title different to the actual qualification, and state why. For instance, it could be due to publicity, advertising, funding and/or for recruitment purposes.

Q61 Review the requirements and related procedures you must follow to ensure that assessment is effective.

Your response should specify all the relevant requirements and procedures which support your subject, for example:

● documentation: assessment plans, reviews, feedback and tracking records, etc. with guidelines for their use;

● relevant legislation such as the Health and Safety at Work Act (1974), Data Protection Act (2003), Equality Act (2010);

● relevant policies and procedures within your own organisation such as appeals, assessment, complaints, confidentiality, marking and feedback, quality assurance, etc;

- requirements such as record keeping, documents and forms to be used, storage periods and security locations, etc;

- the types of assessment activities you will use such as assignments and the supporting grading criteria;

- the Awarding Organisation's requirements for assessing and quality assuring your subject;

- the Sector Skills Council's assessment strategy for your subject;

- your job description or role requirements.

At level 4, in addition to the above, you should read relevant textbooks, articles and journals, and access appropriate websites, referring to them in your response. When writing, you should be analytical rather than descriptive and use a recognised academic style of writing.

For example, you could review the stages of the assessment cycle (see Chapter 7, Question 43 Figure 7.1) and state how the requirements and related procedures you have specified impact upon each stage. For instance, they may hinder rather than support certain aspects. You could also state how areas could be improved, for example you might feel the assessment documentation needs updating, if so, state how and why.

> Level 3 – 5.2 Conduct and record assessments which meet the requirements of the learning programme and the organisation including, where appropriate, the requirements of external bodies
>
> Level 4 – 5.2 Conduct and record assessments which meet the requirements of the learning programme and the organisation including, where appropriate, the requirements of external bodies

Q62 Conduct an assessment activity with your learners which meets the requirements of the learning programme.

This is a practical task to enable you to carry out an assessment activity with your learners in your specialist subject. You should ensure you have the required assessment materials and that your learners are aware of what is involved. The assessment materials and activities you use, for example an assignment, should be written in such a way as to assess skills, knowledge and/or attitudes towards the criteria of the learning programme. You should agree an assessment plan beforehand with your learners, and you may need to liaise with others, for example your learner's employer if the assessment will be in the workplace. You also need to ensure the environment is appropriate and you have all the necessary resources.

Once you have prepared everything, you need to carry out the assessment activity in accordance with the requirements of the learning programme. You might be observed carrying out this task as part of the CTLLS assessment requirements. If this is the case, you should receive a copy of your assessor's checklist or report which you could use as evidence.

At level 4, in addition to the above, you should read relevant textbooks, articles and journals, and access appropriate websites, referring to them in your response. When writing, you should be analytical rather than descriptive and use a recognised academic style of writing.

For example, you could analyse how the assessment activity was for both you and your learners. Did anything go wrong or would you change anything for next time? If you were observed by your CTLLS assessor, you could evaluate the feedback you received.

Q63 What would influence your judgement and decision as to whether the activity has met the requirements of the programme, your organisation and external bodies?

Your response should take into account all the factors which could influence your judgement and decision, such as the following.

- Appeals and complaints – if a learner has made an appeal or complained about a decision you have made, you should not feel you need to pass them if they have not fully met the qualification requirements and assessment criteria. Make sure you follow your organisation's procedures and maintain relevant documents.

- Awarding Organisation – have you understood all their requirements for assessment of the qualification?

- Consistency – are you being fair to all your learners or are you biased towards some learners more than others?

- Methods of assessment – can you differentiate by using an alternative method, for example professional discussion rather than written questions for a dyslexic learner?

- Plagiarism – some learners may have copied work from others or the internet, or not referenced their research adequately. You could type a sentence into a search engine to see if it already exists elsewhere.

- Policies, procedures and codes of practice – are you fully familiar with all the relevant requirements of your organisation for your subject?

- Pressure – do you feel under pressure to pass learners who are borderline, perhaps due to funding measures, retention and achievement targets, inspectors or employer expectations?

- Quality assurance – are you familiar with all the requirements within your organisation for your subject?

- Risk assessments – are any of your learners likely to leave, or do they need extra support for any reason?

- Standardisation – you should standardise your decisions with other assessors of your subject to ensure you are all interpreting the criteria in the same way and being fair and consistent with your decisions.

- The qualification requirements and assessment criteria – have these clearly been met by the learner? Have both you and your learner appropriately interpreted the requirements and criteria?

- Trends – is there a pattern, i.e. are most learners making the same mistakes? If so, it could be that they have misinterpreted something. If this is the case, you could summarise these trends and give a copy to your learners, including aspects of good practice to further their development.

- Type of assessment: formal or informal assessments – you might be more lenient with informal assessments to encourage motivation if the results do not count towards a formal assessment of achievement.

- VACSR – is your learner's evidence valid, authentic, current, sufficient and reliable? How can you ensure their work meets all these points? If you are assessing group work how do you know what each individual has contributed?

If you are in any doubt, you must talk to someone else who is a specialist in your subject area such as your mentor or internal verifier. Samples of your decisions should be checked by your internal verifier to ensure you are assessing correctly and are consistent and fair. However, this usually takes place after you have made a decision and it might be too late if you have made a positive judgement. You will then need to explain to your learner that they have not passed and need to carry out further work. An external verifier from the Awarding Organisation for your subject will also sample your decisions.

At level 4, in addition to the above, you should read relevant textbooks, articles and journals, and access appropriate websites, referring to them in your response. When writing, you should be analytical rather than descriptive and use a recognised academic style of writing.

For example, you could read further regarding assessment and critically analyse quotes such as:

> Assessment should be the tool to celebrate achievement and identify development. In reality it is all too often used as a negative tool to criticise poor achievement or failing standards and, therefore, it is very often seen in a threatening way, because we all fear failure.
>
> (Wilson, 2008, p325)

Q64 What documentation is used during the assessment process with your learners and why?

Your response to this question should include a list of all the documentation you use at your organisation to assess your learners, for example:

- action plans;

- appeals records;

- assessment feedback records;

- assessment grade records;

- assessment plans;

- diagnostic test results;

- initial assessment results;

- learning styles test results;

- observation reports and checklists;

- progress reports to employers or parents/guardians;

- records of achievement;

- skills audit results;

- tracking sheets;

- tutorial review records;

- witness testimonies.

You should ensure you are familiar with the procedures for each of the documents you have listed. Evidence could include anonymised examples of records you have completed.

The reasons for using each of the documents you have listed should be stated, for example an assessment plan should be agreed with each learner prior to any assessment taking place. It should state what will be assessed, by whom, when and where, and how the assessment activity will take place, for example an observation or assignment. If one was not agreed, both the assessor and the learner would not know what was to take place or when.

Records must be maintained to satisfy your organisation's internal quality assurance systems, as well as external regulators such as Ofsted and the Awarding Organisation's requirements. Assessment records must show an audit trail of your learners' progress from commencement to completion and are usually kept at your organisation for three years. If a learner loses their work, without any assessment records you have nothing to show that you actually assessed it. If you are teaching a programme which does not lead to a formal qualification, i.e. is non-accredited, you will still need to record learner progress. This is known as *recognising and recording progress and achievement (RARPA).* It is important to your learner and the funding agencies (if applicable) that achievement is recognised whether or not the programme is accredited.

Records must be up to date, accurate, factual and legible whether they are stored manually or electronically. If you are saving to a computer always ensure you have a backup copy in case any data is lost. You must always maintain confidentiality and follow relevant legislation such as the Data Protection Act (2003), which is mandatory for all organisations that hold or process personal data. The Freedom of Information Act (2000) gives your learners the opportunity to request to see the information your organisation holds about them. Keeping full and accurate factual records is also necessary in case one of your learners appeals against an assessment decision. If this happens, do not take it personally; they will be appealing against your decision, not you.

At level 4, in addition to the above, you should read relevant textbooks, articles and journals, and access appropriate websites, referring to them in your response. When writing, you should be analytical rather than descriptive and use a recognised academic style of writing.

For example, you could evaluate the records you use in relation to the assessment cycle (see Chapter 7, Question 43, Figure 7.1) and recommend modifications and improvements.

Level 3 – 5.3 Communicate relevant assessment information to those with a legitimate interest in learner achievement

Level 4 – 5.3 Communicate relevant assessment information to those with a legitimate interest in learner achievement

---

Q65 Who has a legitimate interest in your learners' achievement besides yourself?

Your response should include all persons and stakeholders such as:

- Awarding Organisation – accountability for your subject decisions;

- colleagues who also come into contact with your learners;

- employers – if your learners are employed or partaking in work experience;

- funding providers;

- inspectors such as Ofsted;

- internal/external verifiers and moderators;

- line managers or supervisors who monitor your progress as a teacher and statistics relating to your learners such as retention and achievement;

- mentor – the person supporting you regarding your subject and teaching in general;

- staff responsible for policies and procedures such as appeals, complaints and quality assurance.

At level 4, in addition to the above, you should read relevant textbooks, articles and journals, and access appropriate websites, referring to them in your response. When writing, you should be analytical rather than descriptive and use a recognised academic style of writing.

For example, you could justify why each of the persons and stakeholders you have listed has a legitimate interest in your learners. For instance, the Awarding Organisation must be able to satisfy themselves that you have interpreted and assessed the qualification requirements correctly. They will want to know that you are suitably qualified and experienced in your specialist subject and are keeping up to date with currency of practice.

Q66 How do you communicate relevant assessment information to them?

Your response should include how you communicate appropriately with each of the persons and stakeholders you have listed in question 65, as in the following examples.

- Awarding Organisation – you will need to check if all communication should go via your internal verifier or moderator, or whether you can contact your external verifier or moderator direct by e-mail, letter or telephone. You may come into contact with them directly if they are inspecting your records or observing your practice.

- Colleagues – in person within your organisation, by e-mail or telephone, or as part of a formal meeting.

- Employers – in person when visiting their organisation or by e-mail, letter or telephone.

- Funding providers – you would probably not contact them directly but communicate with the appropriate contact within your organisation.

- Inspectors – as above; however, you may come into contact with them directly if they are inspecting your records or observing your practice.

- Internal and external verifiers and moderators – as above.

- Line managers or supervisors – in person within your organisation, by e-mail or telephone, or as part of a formal meeting.

- Mentor – in person within your organisation, by e-mail or telephone, or as part of a formal meeting.

- Staff responsible for policies and procedures – in person within your organisation, by e-mail or telephone, or as part of a formal meeting.

No matter how you communicate, whether informally such as by e-mail, or formally such as during a meeting, you should always remain professional and not let personal issues affect the communication process. You could include copies of e-mails and other correspondence as evidence. (Please see Chapter 4 for further details regarding communication.)

At level 4, in addition to the above, you should read relevant textbooks, articles and journals, and access appropriate websites, referring to them in your response. When writing, you should be analytical rather than descriptive and use a recognised academic style of writing.

For example, you could justify why you would communicate with the persons and stakeholders you have listed, perhaps producing a case study of an instance where you had to make contact for a particular reason. You could also justify the difference between communication methods. For example, you might feel using text messages with your external verifier is too informal, is inappropriate and does not maintain a formal record of contact.

Theory focus

References and further information

Flood A, Murray W and Rowell, G (2009) *Authenticity: A guide for teachers.* Coventry: Ofqual

Gravells A (2011) *Principles and Practice of Assessment in the Lifelong Learning Sector.* (2nd edition). Exeter: Learning Matters

Wilson L (2008) *Practical teaching: a guide to PTLLS and CTLLS.* London: Cengage Learning

Websites

Data Protection Act – regulatorylaw.co.uk/Data_Protection_Act_2003.html

Equality Act – www.opsi.gov.uk/si/si2010/uksi_20101736_en_1

Freedom of Information Act – www.opsi.gov.uk/Acts/acts2000/ukpga_20000036 _en_1

Health & Safety at Work Act – www.hse.gov.uk/legislation/hswa.htm

Ofsted – www.ofsted.gov.uk

Plagiarism – www.plagiarism.org

Plagiarism checker – www.plagiarismchecker.com

RARPA – www.ladder4learning.org.uk/resources/learning/rarpa

CHAPTER 12
HOW TO EVALUATE THE EFFECTIVENESS OF OWN PRACTICE

This chapter is in two parts. The first part, *Self-assessment activities*, contains questions and activities which relate to the sixth learning outcome of the CTLLS mandatory unit: *Principles and Practice of Assessment in the Lifelong Learning Sector – Understand how to evaluate the effectiveness of own practice.*

The assessment criteria for each level are shown in boxes and are followed by activities and questions for you to carry out. Ensure your responses are *specific to you*, the *subject* you will teach and the *context* and *environment* in which you will teach.

After completing the activities and questions, check your responses with the second part: *Guidance for evidencing competence*. This guidance is not intended to give you the answers to questions you may be asked in any formal assessments; however, it will help you focus your responses towards meeting the CTLLS requirements.

Self-assessment activities

Level 3 – 6.1 Reflect on the effectiveness of own practice taking account of the views of learners

Level 4 – 6.1 Evaluate the effectiveness of own practice taking account of the views of learners

Q67 Reflect on the effectiveness of your own practice as an assessor.

Q68 How can you obtain the views of your learners regarding the assessment process?

Q69 How will these views impact upon your own practice as an assessor?

Q70 What CPD could you undertake to improve your role as an assessor?

Guidance for evidencing competence

Level 3 – 6.1 Reflect on the effectiveness of own practice taking account of the views of learners

Level 4 – 6.1 Evaluate the effectiveness of own practice taking account of the views of learners

Q67 Reflect on the effectiveness of your own practice as an assessor.

To reflect upon the effectiveness of your practice as an assessor, you need to consider your role throughout the whole process of the assessment cycle, for example how you managed initial assessment, assessment planning, assessment activities, making decisions, giving feedback and reviewing progress with your learners (see Chapter 7, question 43, Figure 7.1). You should consider feedback you have received from others involved in the assessment process, for example your internal/external moderator/verifier. The reports that are received from the Awarding Organisation should be disseminated to all assessors and you could refer to their feedback when evaluating your practice. You might have participated in standardisation activities to compare your decisions with others, in which case the feedback from these will help you reflect upon the judgements you have made. You should also consider the achievement and success rates of your learners. If your figures are low, is this because your learners were taking a programme they were not capable of achieving (due to an inadequate initial assessment)? Or could it be some other reason? If so, you need to reflect what has been happening and what you can do to improve the situation.

You might have been writing a reflective learning journal throughout your time on the CTLLS programme and you could refer to this in your response. Perhaps you consider yourself a good assessor because you follow all procedures, are objective with decisions and maintain good records. However, you might not feel confident about giving face-to-face feedback in case a learner becomes confrontational. This therefore could be an area for you to reflect upon to aid your development.

At level 4, in addition to the above, you should read relevant textbooks, articles and journals, and access appropriate websites, referring to them in your response. When writing, you should be analytical rather than descriptive and use a recognised academic style of writing.

For example, you could evaluate the effectiveness of your practice by relating to reflective theorists such as: Brookfield (1995), Gibbs (1988), Griffiths and Tann (1992), Kolb (1984) Schön (1983) and others. You could also compare and contrast different theories.

Q68 How can you obtain the views of your learners regarding the assessment process?

Obtaining the views of your learners will greatly assist you when reflecting upon your role as an assessor. You can gain these views formally and/or informally. Whichever method you use, you should always inform your learners about how their feedback will lead to actions and improvements, otherwise they might not take the process seriously. You could ask your learners directly after an assessment what they felt about the process. However, although some learners might feel confident enough to tell you, others might not.

The response to question 40 in Chapter 6 gives details of how to obtain feedback. You may be able to cross reference some of your evidence from this question as part of your response.

At level 4, in addition to the above, you should read relevant textbooks, articles and journals, and access appropriate websites, referring to them in your response. When writing, you should be analytical rather than descriptive and use a recognised academic style of writing.

For example, you could refer to different ways of producing and analysing questionnaires, referencing your response to various theorists, for example Cohen et al (2007) and Denscombe (2002). You could also provide evidence of questionnaires or surveys you have used with your learners, along with a summary of the responses and any action required.

Q69 How will these views impact upon your own practice as an assessor?

When evaluating your own practice, you need to consider the views of your learners and others in order to improve. How you do this will depend upon the type of feedback you have obtained and how useful it will be. A survey might have ascertained that most learners felt the initial assessment could be improved, for example by using a computerised learning styles test rather than a paper-based one. You might have obtained feedback from an individual learner that their assessment plan had unrealistic target dates. In this case, you could renegotiate the plan with more suitable dates. Feedback from your learners might impact upon your role by alerting you to other aspects, for example the types of questions used in an assignment were too complex, some activities might not have been challenging enough, or a multiple choice test confused a dyslexic learner as they mistook a *b* for a *d*.

You will need to ensure the activities you used to assess knowledge, skills and attitudes were valid and reliable, and that you only assessed the criteria you were meant to assess. You will also need to evaluate if the assessment types and methods you used were successful. You will need to ask yourself if you assessed fairly, or gave some learners more help than others. The views of your learners and others should have an impact upon your own role by helping you improve the assessment experience. You might consider creating a best practice checklist for assessors which could include tips and advice. This would ensure all assessors are giving a professional, fair and standardised service to everyone involved in the assessment process.

At level 4, in addition to the above, you should read relevant textbooks, articles and journals, and access appropriate websites, referring to them in your response. When writing, you should be analytical rather than descriptive and use a recognised academic style of writing.

For example, you could evaluate how you can improve your role as an assessor in particular areas, and critically analyse quotes from relevant textbooks, such as:

> It is important at the start of any study of assessment of student learning that you recognise the distinction between two types of assessment: formative and summative. The distinction between assessment to satisfy the needs of society ('summative' assessment) and assessment to help in both teaching and learning ('formative' assessment).

> (Reece and Walker, 2007, p323)

You could also explain how you standardise your practice with other assessors, and how verification and moderation activities help ensure you are assessing fairly and consistently.

Q70 What CPD could you undertake to improve your role as an assessor?

When deciding upon CPD activities, don't just think about attending events or taking qualifications. Instead, ask yourself what would be most effective for developing yourself as an assessor, which will lead to an improvement in your practice and ultimately impact positively on your learners.

You could observe or talk to your mentor or another assessor in your subject area to see how they carry out the aspects of the assessment cycle. You could also ask your mentor or a colleague to observe your assessment practice and give you feedback. You might have been observed, as part of your organisation's quality assurance system, by an inspector and/or an internal or external verifier or moderator. Their feedback should help you decide what CPD you might need, and give you advice for improvement. Reading textbooks and journals can help improve your knowledge and you could sign up for and read regular newsletters and updates from appropriate websites.

You should have registered with the IfL by now. If not, go to their website (www.ifl.ac.uk) and do this. You might want to update your curriculum vitae so that you have all your qualifications and experience to hand as you will need to input this when registering. The IfL will monitor your CPD as you must achieve a certain number of hours per year depending upon your job role. You can keep records of your CPD manually or electronically, or even via the IfL's e-portfolio called *Reflect*.

The practice of assessment has been recognised as a professional activity by the granting of Chartered Status to the Institute of Educational Assessors (CIEA). Their aim is to improve the quality of assessment in schools and colleges by working with educational assessors to develop their knowledge, understanding and capability in all aspects of educational testing and assessment.

Examples of CPD include:

- attending events;
- attending meetings and standardisation activities, and making a significant input;
- e-learning activities;
- evaluating feedback;
- joining professional associations or committees and networking;
- peer observations;
- research regarding assessment processes and practice;
- researching developments or changes to your subject and/or legislation;
- secondments;
- self-reflection;
- subscribing to relevant journals and magazines;
- taking further qualifications;
- visits to other organisations;
- voluntary work;
- writing or reviewing books and articles; and anything else that is realistic and relevant to your assessment role.

You could create an action plan for yourself to show what CPD activities you will undertake.

At level 4, in addition to the above, you should read relevant textbooks, articles and journals, and access appropriate websites, referring to them in your response. When writing, you should be analytical rather than descriptive and use a recognised academic style of writing.

For example, you could partake in relevant CPD and evaluate its impact upon your role as an assessor. You could refer to relevant textbooks such as Hitching (2008) who states: *Effective CPD is highly personalised with critical reflection leading us to consider what we do well, what we do less well and how we develop both for the benefit of ourselves and our learners.*

You could also carry out a SWOT analysis (strengths, weaknesses, opportunities and threats) regarding your practice.

Theory focus

References and further information

Brookfield S (1995) *Becoming a Critically Reflective Teacher.* San Francisco: Jossey Bass

Cohen L, Manion L and Morrison K (2007) *Research Methods in Education.* London: Routledge

Denscombe M (2002) *Ground Rules for Good Research.* Buckingham: Open University Press

Gibbs G (1988) *Learning by doing: a guide to teaching and learning methods.* Oxford: Further Education Unit

Gravells A (2011) *Principles and Practice of Assessment in the Lifelong Learning Sector* (2nd edition). Exeter: Learning Matters

Griffiths M and Tann S (1992) Using reflective practice to link personal and public theories. *Journal of Education for Teaching,* 18(1)

Hitching J (2008) *Maintaining Your Licence to Practise.* Exeter: Learning Matters

Kolb D (1984) *Experiential Learning: Experience as the Source of Learning and Development.* New Jersey: Prentice-Hall

Reece I and Walker S (2007) *Teaching Training and Learning: a practical guide* (6th edition). Tyne and Wear: Business Education Publishers Ltd

Roffey-Barentsen J and Malthouse R (2009) *Reflective Practice in the Lifelong Learning Sector.* Exeter: Learning Matters

Schön D (1983) *The Reflective Practitioner.* San Francisco: Jossey-Bass

Tummons J (2010) *Becoming a Professional Tutor in the Lifelong Learning Sector* (2nd edition). Exeter: Learning Matters

Wallace S and Gravells J (2007) *Mentoring.* Exeter: Learning Matters

Wood J and Dickinson J (2011) *Quality Assurance and Evaluation in the Lifelong Learning Sector.* Exeter: Learning Matters

Websites

Chartered Institute of Educational Assessors – www.ciea.org.uk

Institute for Learning – www.ifl.ac.uk

Reflective practice – www.learningandteaching.info/learning/reflecti.htm

SWOT analysis – www.businessballs.com/swotanalysisfreetemplate.htm

CHAPTER 13
THE CTLLS QUALIFICATION

Introduction

In this chapter you will learn about the:

- PTLLS unit;

- CTLLS mandatory and optional units;

- minimum core;

- teaching practice;

- observed practice.

The PTLLS unit

The Preparing to Teach in the Lifelong Learning Sector (PTLLS) unit is mandatory and should be the first unit taken as part of the Certificate in Teaching in the Lifelong Learning Sector (CTLLS) qualification. Alternatively, it can be achieved prior to commencing CTLLS, whether at the same organisation as you are taking CTLLS, or elsewhere. It is an award in its own right and can be thought of as a *threshold licence to teach*. It can be taken at level 3 or level 4 depending upon your prior knowledge and experience. The difference between the levels is expressed in the assessment criteria, enabling you to meet the requirements at an appropriate level. For example, if you are aiming for level 3 you will *explain* how you do something, at level 4 you will *analyse* why you do it. If you are aiming for level 4 you will need to carry out relevant research, reference your work to theorists and use an academic style of writing.

There are five learning outcomes which you will need to successfully evidence to achieve the PTLLS Award:

1. understand own role, responsibilities and boundaries of role in relation to teaching;

2. understand appropriate teaching and learning approaches in the specialist area;

3. demonstrate session planning skills;

4. understand how to deliver inclusive sessions which motivate learners;

5. understand the use of different assessment methods and the need for record keeping.

The content of the unit will be the same no matter where you are studying; however, the assessment requirements may differ depending upon which Awarding Organisation you are registered with and which level you are taking.

The evidence you could provide includes:

- assessment tasks – theory and practical;

- assignments;

- work products, for example session plans and resources;

- observation records of your micro-teach or teaching practice;

- professional discussion record;

- reflective learning journals;

- responses to written questions;

- self-evaluations.

Once you have achieved the PTLLS unit, you can progress to the mandatory and optional units of CTLLS.

CTLLS mandatory and optional units

The CTLLS qualification can be achieved at either level 3 or level 4, just like the PTLLS Award. However, CTLLS is made up of mandatory and optional units so the correct combination of units and levels must be met to achieve the desired level. You will need to discuss this carefully with your assessor to ensure you are working towards the correct combination.

Mandatory units

Once you have achieved your PTLLS unit, you will take two further mandatory units which are:

- Planning and Enabling Learning in the Lifelong Learning Sector;

- Principles and Practice of Assessment in the Lifelong Learning Sector.

Both these units can be achieved at level 3 or 4. The chapters in this book will help you identify relevant evidence for assessment at each level.

If your teaching role changes after completing the CTLLS qualification, you will need to take the Diploma in Teaching in the Lifelong Learning Sector (DTLLS) qualification (also known as the Certificate in Education or Post Graduate

Certificate in Education). You should be able to carry forward the PTLLS and Planning and Enabling Learning mandatory units and possibly some optional units that you have achieved. However, you will need to discuss this with your assessor as there may be a requirement that you achieve these units at level 4.

Optional units

There are many optional units available at level 3 and/or 4 which can be taken as part of the CTLLS qualification. You should choose units which are part of your job role or will help enhance and improve it.

Table 13.1 lists some of the units current at the time of publication. You will need to discuss with your assessor which ones will be appropriate as some units cannot be combined with others. This is known as *rules of combination*. For example, if you choose to take the *Preparing for the coaching role* unit you cannot take *The coaching and mentoring roles* unit as they are very similar.

Table 13.1 Examples of CTLLS optional units (listed alphabetically)

Title of optional unit*	Level*
Assessment and support for the recognition of prior learning through the accreditation of learning outcomes	3
Conflict management training	3
Delivering employability skills	4
Developing and managing resources in the lifelong learning sector	4
Equality and diversity	3 or 4
Evaluating learning programmes	4
Inclusive practice	4
Learning in the community	4
Managing and responding to behaviours in a learning environment	4
Managing behaviours in the learning environment	4
Planning and assessing for inclusive practice (ESOL)	4
Preparing for the coaching role	3 or 4
Preparing for the mentoring role	3 or 4
Preparing learners for e-testing	3
Preparing to use e-learning and e-assessment in the lifelong learning sector	4
Principles and practice of instructional techniques	4
Professional development planning	4
Professional practice skills	4
Specialist delivery techniques and activities	4

Teaching a specialist subject	4
The coaching and mentoring roles	3 or 4
Working with individuals and groups in the learning environment	4
Working with the 14–16 age range in the learning environment	4

*correct at time of publication

The minimum core

The *minimum core* is the term used to refer to the basic standards of literacy, language, numeracy and ICT that should be demonstrated by all teachers in the Lifelong Learning Sector in order to support learning.

Achievement of the *Planning and Enabling Learning in the Lifelong Learning Sector* unit requires you to demonstrate and evidence all these skills to at least level 2. However, it is not just about demonstrating your own skills in these areas; it is about being able to develop these skills in your learners too. Part of successful achievement of the PTLLS unit requires you to embed aspects of English, maths and ICT into your teaching sessions. These are known as *Functional Skills*. These are the skills that enable individuals to work confidently, effectively and independently throughout life.

You might like to take additional training in the minimum core areas, for example if your computer skills need further development or you feel your spelling and/or grammar and numerical skills need improving. When teaching, your learners will trust and believe you; if you are spelling words wrongly your learners will think the spelling is correct, just because you are their teacher.

To evidence the minimum core, you will need to show that you have the required knowledge, understanding and personal skills for each area, as in the following examples.

- Literacy and language – you should have knowledge about language and of the four skills of speaking, listening, reading and writing and be able to show you understand these by putting them into practice. Demonstrating your personal skills will be shown by the way you communicate with your learners (verbally and non-verbally), how you respond to situations, what reference and support materials you use and how you convey your literacy, i.e. using accurate spelling, grammar and punctuation in written text. Evidence you could provide includes your scheme of work, session plans, activities you have designed for learners, resource materials, handouts and presentations.
- Numeracy – you should have knowledge about numerical communication and processes and be able to show you understand these by putting them into practice. Demonstrating your personal skills will be shown by how you communicate with others regarding numeracy (to support your job role and your learners), and how you use processes such as analysing data, making calculations

and solving problems. Evidence you could provide includes statistical analysis, reports, retention, achievement and success data and financial calculations.

- ICT – you should have knowledge about information communication technology and processes and be able to show you understand these by putting them into practice. Demonstrating your personal skills will be shown by how you communicate with others in a variety of ways and how you use ICT systems to support teaching and learning. Evidence you could provide includes practical examples of using ICT such as e-mails, presentation equipment, software packages, a VLE and documents you have produced electronically such as handouts or interactive activities.

You may be able to use recognised qualifications as evidence towards the minimum core of literacy, language and numeracy which you have already achieved. For example:

- Key Skills in Communication at level 2 or above;

- Ordinary (O) level or GCSE English (A*–C);

- Functional Skills in Maths at level 2 or above;

- O level or GCSE mathematics (A*–C) or CSE Grade I mathematics.

Standards Verification UK (SVUK) is the body responsible for endorsing initial teacher training qualifications for the Lifelong Learning sector in England and Wales. You can view their list of approved recognised literacy and numeracy qualifications via the SVUK website or by using the shortcut: tiny.cc/4q4l4

You should create opportunities during the teaching and learning process to demonstrate all aspects of the minimum core. For more detailed information, please refer to the documents LLUK (2007a) and LLUK (2007b) listed at the end of this chapter. The minimum core standards LLUK (2007a) can be accessed via the LLUK website or by using the shortcut tinyurl.com/6zmwcg. When you look at the standards you will see that language and literacy are combined, and each area has a *Part A* and a *Part B*. Part A refers to the knowledge and understanding that you should gain, and Part B refers to the personal skills that you should demonstrate during your teaching.

Teaching practice

Throughout your time working towards CTLLS, you will need to demonstrate you can put theory into practice by evidencing at least 30 hours of teaching practice. This teaching should be with your own learners in a recognised lifelong learning context. You must use a range of inclusive and differentiated learning techniques and integrate the minimum core throughout your delivery. You should keep a log of at least 30 hours of teaching practice activities and cross reference these to your supporting evidence as in Table 13.2 below. The evidence you provide should include all the documentation and resources you have used to deliver your sessions, along with your assessor's observation reports. You should carry out a self-evaluation after each session you have taught, taking into account your strengths, areas for development, and any actions or improvements required. If you are taking the CTLLS qualification at level 4, you should be analytical rather than descriptive when writing these and make reference to theories of teaching and learning.

Table 13.2 Log of teaching practice

Date and time	Number of learners and subject	Location	Length of session	Evidence reference
5 October 3 p.m.	15 Level 2 Certificate in Customer Service	Room 7 Main building	2 hours	1 – scheme of work 2 – session plan 3 – handout 4 – self-evaluation form
9 November 3 p.m.	15 Level 2 Certificate in Customer Service	Room 7 Main building	2 hours	5 – session plan 6 – handout 7 – copy of presentation 8 – self-evaluation form
10 November 7 p.m.	12 Level 1 Award in IT User Skills	Room 1 ICT building	1.5 hours	9 – scheme of work 10 – session plan 11 – handout 12– activity 13 – self-evaluation form 14 – assessor's observation report

While working towards the CTLLS qualification, you should have a mentor – someone who is qualified and experienced in your specialist subject who can give you support and advice. It would be beneficial for you to observe one of their sessions and to ask them to observe one or more of your sessions. This process should help you gain new ideas regarding teaching your own subject. You might also like to observe your colleagues or peers who teach different subjects to help you appreciate other ways of how teaching and learning can take place. Being observed by others before you are formally observed by your CTLLS assessor should help you relax a little when the time comes for a formal observation.

Micro-teaching

As part of the PTLLS unit, you are required to deliver a short session to your current learners (if you are in-service) or to your peers; the latter is known as micro-teaching and enables you to demonstrate your teaching skills in a safe environment. You might also be required to deliver a short session to your peers for an aspect of the CTLLS mandatory units of *Planning and Enabling Learning in the Lifelong Learning Sector*, and *Principles and Practice of Assessment in the Lifelong Learning Sector*. For example, you might be asked to research *How to integrate*

Functional Skills into your specialist subject and then deliver a short session regarding your findings to your peers. If this is the case, you should write a rationale and methodology for your research and a precis of your findings afterwards. Do check with your assessor if there is a wordcount for these and make sure you are within 10 per cent above or below it. The process you go through to research your subject is extremely important, as you will be assessed on this as well as the session you deliver. Make sure you prepare a session plan in advance of your delivery to help you remain focussed.

Your assessor might make a visual recording of your session which you can view in your own time. This will enable you to see things you were not aware of, for example saying *erm*, using a lot of hand gestures or not using much eye contact. You should be told in advance if you are being recorded. Try not to be put off by it, but embrace it as a way of developing yourself further. Any micro-teaching sessions you deliver cannot be included as part of your 30 hours of teaching practice.

Rationale and methodology

Think of the rationale as *what* you are doing and *why*. The methodology is *how* you will carry this out. For example:

> For my *Planning and Enabling Learning unit*, I will be researching the topic of how to integrate Functional Skills within my specialist subject of plumbing. I will be focussing on how I can enable my learners to use the skills of English, maths and ICT without thinking of them as separate subjects. I would like my learners to increase their skills in these areas, at the same time as learning the subject of plumbing. My methodology is to research information about Functional Skills from government and other websites, read published documents, relevant textbooks and journals, and talk to other plumbing teachers. I will then create a precis of my findings and include evidence of my research.

Precis

Your precis should be a summary of your findings and research, for example a word-processed report regarding how you approached the research, along with a review of the information you obtained from your web searches, documents, textbooks, journals and discussions. You could use subheadings for each aspect of your report such as:

- introduction and rationale, i.e. the reason for your research;
- methodology, i.e. the methods you used and why (which might be different from your original ideas);
- findings, i.e. a review of the research you undertook;
- conclusion, i.e. how your findings are significant to teaching and learning, any changes you will make as a result and any further action you will carry out.

The evidence to support your research could include extracts from textbooks and journals, printouts from the internet, cuttings from newspapers, notes of discussions, a bibliography and reference list. Rather than provide the original textbooks or journals, you could photocopy relevant pages and highlight the significant parts, making critical notes of the impact upon teaching and learning. It is quality not quantity that counts; do not duplicate or include too much evidence and check you are not breaching copyright when photocopying books or journals.

You might be required to deliver a micro-teach session to your peers regarding your findings. Prior to your delivery you should create a session plan consisting of an introduction, main content and summary. This should be concise to enable coverage within the time, which might only be 15 minutes. However, consider what you could remove should you overrun time, or what you could add in if you find you have spare time, for example using open questions. You should also prepare all your resources, such as a presentation, and have the evidence of your research and your report to hand.

After you have delivered your session, you should receive feedback from your CTLLS assessor and your peers. You should then evaluate how you felt your session went by completing a self-evaluation form or writing a reflective learning journal. This should focus on your strengths, areas for development, and action and improvements required.

Observed practice

You will be formally observed on at least three occasions throughout your time taking the CTLLS qualification. This should be by your CTLLS assessor. However, at some point you might also be observed by your mentor, a colleague, an internal verifier and/or an external inspector from an Awarding Organisation. It would be valuable beforehand to see their observation form or the checklist that they will be using; this way you will have a good idea of what they are looking for. The feedback you receive afterwards from all observed practice should be used to help you reflect upon and develop the teaching and learning process.

Different observers will be looking for different aspects of teaching and learning. Your CTLLS assessor will be observing to see that you achieve the criteria for the qualification. Your mentor will be observing to see how you deliver and assess your specialist subject. A colleague will be observing to see that you are following your organisation's quality assurance procedures for teaching and learning. An external inspector, for example from Ofsted, may appear unannounced and will observe you to see if you are giving a quality experience to your learners. An internal verifier will need to satisfy themselves that you are making valid and reliable assessment decisions. An external verifier from an Awarding Organisation will be observing to see that you are following their regulations and assessing accurately. However, all observers will want to satisfy themselves that you are teaching and assessing effectively, as well as supporting your learners towards the achievement of their learning programme or qualification.

Being observed, even if you are an experienced teacher, can be traumatic or stressful as you will want to deliver a perfect session. However, you are being observed by your own learners every time you teach, but they do not always give you formal feedback after each session. If you are nervous, do not let your learners know as they probably will not notice. You are human though and if you make a mistake, your observer will be watching to see that you put it right. Afterwards, they will give you feedback along with helpful advice as to how you could approach things differently in the future.

Preparing for your observation

You should be notified in advance when the observation will take place and how long your observer will stay. Your session might last longer than the time your observer will be present, so they might miss the beginning or ending and arrive part way through. If possible, you should try and plan the session to allow you time to talk to your observer either before, afterwards or preferably both.

You might want to inform your learners in advance that the session is to be observed, but that you expect them to behave in their usual way. Otherwise, they might feel they should be quiet, not ask any questions or ask too many questions to appear helpful, which will give a false impression of what normally occurs. Your assessor may want to talk to your learners at some point, and might ask you to leave the room while they do this. Do not be concerned as this is quite normal; they like to find out what your learners are experiencing and how your teaching is having an impact upon their learning.

Make sure all the materials you have prepared are of good quality, address inclusivity and differentiation, and are free from spelling, grammar and punctuation errors. Do not try and prepare too much, or use any equipment you are not totally comfortable with. Always have a contingency plan, i.e. hard copies of a presentation in case the computer stops working.

Check the environment and equipment beforehand and complete any health and safety checks or risk assessments. Make sure you have enough of everything for the number of learners you expect and be prepared by remaining focussed and following your session plan. Make sure you have a clear aim with objectives or learning outcomes for your learners to achieve.

The observation

Your assessor will probably arrive early to talk to you beforehand about the observation process, the documentation they will be completing and to arrange when they will give you feedback. They may choose where they want to sit, or you could place a chair in an appropriate place for them where they can see everything.

The session you are delivering may be one of many, for which you will have a scheme of work to follow. You should give a copy of this, along with your session plan, to your observer. You might want to give them details of individual learners to show you are differentiating your teaching to meet their needs and addressing inclusivity. They may want to see your register, delivery materials and assessment documentation. Try not to look at your observer while they are with you; they are not part of your group and will not participate in any activities. They will be making lots of notes throughout the session so try not to be concerned if they do not appear to be watching you all the time; they will still be listening to what is going on. If you can, forget that they are there and ignore them; your learners should be the focus of your session not your assessor.

You could introduce your assessor to your learners and state they are observing the session, not the learners as individuals. Having a stranger in the room might lead to some behaviour issues if you have not forewarned your learners. If so, you must deal with these as soon as they arise and in a professional manner. Just be yourself and if you are asked a question you do not know the answer to, say you will find out, and then make sure you do.

Your assessor might be seeing the very first session of a programme, in which case you will have several administrative duties to perform, including an induction to the programme, icebreaker and the setting of ground rules. If you are being observed during one of several sessions, you will need to take the register and include a link to the last session with time for learner questions or a starter activity at the beginning. Make sure you start promptly, remain in control and are organised.

Keep your session plan handy. You could highlight key points which you can glance at to make sure you are keeping to your timings and order of delivery. You may find that you rush things as you are nervous and lose track of the timings in your plan. If so, have a spare activity that you could give your learners to fill in some time. Depending upon the level of your learners you could give them a crossword or they could have a small group discussion regarding the pros and cons of a relevant topic.

Ensure your learners are engaged throughout and that they are learning. Ask lots of open questions to different learners, by name, to check their knowledge. You could have a list of your learners' names and tick them off once you have asked a question or involved them at some point. Use a variety of teaching and learning approaches to address all learning styles, create opportunities for small group work, encourage peer support and set challenging activities for higher level learners. If possible, use new technology to support the learning process such as an interactive whiteboard or a VLE.

At the end of your session you need to link to the next session (if applicable) and set any homework or extension activities. Before your learners leave the room, make sure they tidy their work areas. Always plan to finish on time otherwise your learners might decide to leave before you have completed. If the room needs to be left tidy, involve your learners in this before the session finishes. You can then talk to your assessor after your learners have left, providing time has been arranged for this.

After your observation

Your observer should give you verbal feedback as soon as possible after the session when your learners have left. Ideally, this should be in a quiet area which will enable you to listen and focus upon what they are saying. Hopefully, the feedback you receive will reassure you that you are teaching correctly and that learning is taking place. However, if you receive some negative feedback do not take it personally; your assessor has only seen a snapshot of what you are capable of. You might be given a grade, for example pass or refer. If you receive a refer, you will be given developmental advice and further support to enable you to work towards a pass next time.

Your observer may also ask you some questions about how you felt the session went, and give you feedback from their discussion with your learners (if applicable). You should take the opportunity to ask questions about how you can improve the way learning takes place, or what you could do differently next time. An honest dialogue will prove very useful to your long-term development. You might hear some feedback you do not agree with. Your assessor will have seen your delivery from a different perspective to yourself, therefore do not argue, but ask them to clarify how they made their judgement. It could be that you thought everything was going well but feedback from your learners to your assessor stated otherwise. If you really do not agree with your assessor's decision you could appeal. However, observations are a tool to help you improve your teaching and the learner experience, and you should respect the judgement of your assessor. Arguing with them will not help the situation. If you do appeal, you will need to have good grounds as to why you disagree with their judgement. A further observation date might be arranged to enable your assessor (or an alternative observer) to see if you have improved your knowledge and skills after you have learnt more from the CTLLS programme.

You might want to make notes during the feedback process as you will be receiving a lot of information and may forget some comments afterwards. You should be given a copy of your assessor's report or checklist which you must read carefully and refer to when writing your self-evaluation. You could discuss the observation process and the feedback you gained with your mentor. They might be able to reassure you if you are feeling sensitive afterwards.

The evidence you could provide to support your teaching practice includes:

- action plans/individual learning plans;
- assessment plans, activities, feedback and decision records;
- assessor observation reports or checklists;
- evidence of integrating the minimum core of literacy, language, numeracy and ICT;
- initial assessments;
- notes/e-mails showing liaison with others;
- resources such as copies of presentations, handouts, learner activities, etc.;
- schemes of work;

- self-evaluation reports;

- session plans;

- witness testimonies, i.e. from your mentor.

Successfully completing the teaching practice aspect of the CTLLS qualification will help your motivation to achieve the mandatory and optional units. Once you have achieved these and evidenced the minimum core, you will need to undertake a period of probation, known as professional formation. You can then apply for your teaching status of Associate Teacher Learning and Skills (ATLS) through the IfL. This should be within five years of commencing your qualification, for example when you started the PTLLS unit and registered with the IfL.

Summary

In this chapter you have learnt about the:

- PTLLS unit;

- CTLLS mandatory and optional units;

- minimum core;

- teaching practice;

- observed practice.

Theory focus
References and further information

Duckworth V, Wood J, Bostock J and Dickinson J (2010) *Successful Teaching Practice in the Lifelong Learning Sector*. Exeter: Learning Matters

Francis M and Gould J (2009) *Achieving your PTLLS Award*. London: Sage

Gravells A (2010) *Passing PTLLS Assessments*. Exeter: Learning Matters

Gravells A (2011) *Preparing to Teach in the Lifelong Learning Sector* (4th edition). Exeter: Learning Matters

LLUK (2007a) *Addressing literacy, language, numeracy and ICT needs in education and training: Defining the minimum core of teachers' knowledge,*

understanding and personal skills. London: Lifelong Learning UK

LLUK (2007b) *Literacy, Language, Numeracy and ICT: Inclusive learning approaches for all teachers, tutors and trainers in the learning and skills sector*. London: Lifelong Learning UK

Race P and Pickford R (2007) *Making teaching work*. London: Sage

Williams J (2010) *Study Skills for PTLLS*. Exeter: Learning Matters

Wilson L (2008) *Practical teaching: a guide to PTLLS and CTLLS*. London: Cengage Learning

Websites

Awarding Organisations – www.ofqual.gov.uk/for-awarding-organisations

English and Maths online learning – www.move-on.org.uk

Functional Skills – www.dcsf.gov.uk/14-19/index.cfm?sid=3&pid=225&ctype=None &ptype=Contents

Further Education Teachers' Qualifications (England) Regulations (2007) – www.legislation.gov.uk/uksi/2007/2264/regulation/3/made

Institute for Learning – www.ifl.ac.uk

IT online learning – www.onlinebasics.co.uk

Lifelong Learning UK – www.lluk.org

Minimum Core Standards – tinyurl.com/6zmwcg

Observations of teaching and learning –

www.excellencegateway.org.uk/page.aspx?o=128948

Ofsted – www.ofsted.gov.uk

SVUK approved literacy and numeracy qualifications – tiny.cc/4q4l4

Planning and enabling learning level 3
Criteria and self-audit

Learning outcomes The learner will:	Assessment criteria The learner can:	List of evidence which meets the assessment criteria:	Work required to meet the assessment criteria:
1 Understand ways to negotiate appropriate individual goals with learners	1.1 Explain the role of initial assessment in the learning and teaching process 1.2 Describe different methods of initial assessment for use with learners 1.3 Explain ways of planning, negotiating and recording appropriate learning goals with learners		
2 Understand how to plan for inclusive learning	2.1 Establish and maintain an inclusive learning environment 2.2 Devise a scheme of work which meets learners' needs and curriculum requirements 2.3 Devise session plans which meet the aims and needs of learners 2.4 Explain ways in which session plans can be adapted to the individual needs of learners 2.5 Plan the appropriate use of a variety of delivery methods, explaining the choice 2.6 Identify opportunities for learners to provide feedback to inform practice		

Learning outcomes The learner will:	Assessment criteria The learner can:	List of evidence which meets the assessment criteria:	Work required to meet the assessment criteria:
3 Understand how to use teaching and learning strategies and resources inclusively to meet curriculum requirements	3.1 Use a range of inclusive learning activities to enthuse and motivate learners, ensuring that curriculum requirements are met 3.2 Identify the strengths and limitations of a range of resources, including new and emerging technologies, showing how these resources can be used to promote equality, support diversity and contribute to effective learning 3.3 Identify literacy, language, numeracy and ICT skills which are integral to own specialist area 3.4 Select/adapt and use a range of inclusive resources to promote inclusive learning and teaching		
4 Understand how to use a range of communication skills and methods to communicate effectively with learners and relevant parties in own organisation	4.1 Use different communication methods and skills to meet the needs of learners and the organisation 4.2 Identify ways in which own communication skills could be improved, including an explanation of how barriers to effective communication might be overcome 4.3 Liaise with other relevant parties to effectively meet the needs of learners		
5 Understand and demonstrate knowledge of the minimum core in own practice	5.1 Apply minimum core specifications in literacy to improve own practice 5.2 Apply minimum core specifications in language to improve own practice 5.3 Apply minimum core specifications in mathematics to improve own practice 5.4 Apply minimum core specifications in ICT user skills to improve own practice		
6 Understand how reflection, evaluation and feedback can be used to develop own practice	6.1 Use regular reflection and feedback from others, including learners, to evaluate and improve own practice		

Planning and enabling learning level 4

Criteria and self-audit

Learning outcomes The learner will:	Assessment criteria The learner can:	List of evidence which meets the assessment criteria:	Work required to meet the assessment criteria:
1 Understand ways to negotiate appropriate individual goals with learners	1.1 Analyse the role of initial assessment in the learning and teaching process 1.2 Describe and evaluate different methods of initial assessment for use with learners 1.3 Evaluate ways of planning, negotiating and recording appropriate learning goals with learners		
2 Understand how to plan for inclusive learning	2.1 Establish and maintain an inclusive learning environment 2.2 Devise and justify a scheme of work which meets learners' needs and curriculum requirements 2.3 Devise and justify session plans which meet the aims and needs of individual learners and/or groups 2.4 Analyse ways in which session plans can be adapted to the individual needs of learners 2.5 Plan the appropriate use of a variety of delivery methods, justifying the choice 2.6 Identify and evaluate opportunities for learners to provide feedback to inform practice		

Learning outcomes The learner will:	Assessment criteria The learner can:	List of evidence which meets the assessment criteria:	Work required to meet the assessment criteria:
3 Understand how to use teaching and learning strategies and resources inclusively to meet curriculum requirements	3.1 Select/adapt, use and justify a range of inclusive learning activities to enthuse and motivate learners, ensuring that curriculum requirements are met 3.2 Analyse the strengths and limitations of a range of resources, including new and emerging technologies, showing how these resources can be used to promote equality, support diversity and contribute to effective learning 3.3 Identify literacy, language, numeracy and ICT skills which are integral to own specialist area, reviewing how they support learner achievement 3.4 Select/adapt, use and justify a range of inclusive resources to promote inclusive learning and teaching		
4 Understand how to use a range of communication skills and methods to communicate effectively with learners and relevant parties in own organisation	4.1 Use and evaluate different communication methods and skills to meet the needs of learners and the organisation 4.2 Evaluate own communication skills, identifying ways in which these could be improved including an analysis of how barriers to effective communication might be overcome 4.3 Identify and liaise with appropriate and relevant parties to effectively meet the needs of learners		
5 Understand and demonstrate knowledge of the minimum core in own practice	5.1 Apply minimum core specifications in literacy to improve own practice 5.2 Apply minimum core specifications in language to improve own practice 5.3 Apply minimum core specifications in mathematics to improve own practice 5.4 Apply minimum core specifications in ICT user skills to improve own practice		
6 Understand how reflection, evaluation and feedback can be used to develop own good practice	6.1 Use regular reflection and feedback from others, including learners, to evaluate and improve own practice, making recommendations for modification as appropriate		

Principles and practice of assessment level 3

Criteria and self-audit

Learning outcomes The learner will:	Assessment criteria The learner can:	List of evidence which meets the assessment criteria:	Work required to meet the assessment criteria:
1 Understand key concepts and principles of assessment	1.1 Identify and define the key concepts and principles of assessment		
2 Understand and use different types of assessment	2.1 Explain and demonstrate how different types of assessment can be used effectively to meet the individual needs of learners		
3 Understand the strengths and limitations of a range of assessment methods, including, as appropriate, those which exploit new and emerging technologies	3.1 Identify the strengths and limitations of a range of assessment methods with reference to the needs of particular learners and key concepts and principles of assessment 3.2 Use a range of assessment methods appropriately to ensure that learners produce assessment evidence that is valid, reliable, sufficient, authentic and current 3.3 Explain how the use of peer and self-assessment can be used to promote learner involvement and personal responsibility in the assessment of their learning		
4 Understand the role of feedback and questioning in the assessment of learning	4.1 Explain how feedback and questioning contributes to the assessment process 4.2 Use feedback and questioning effectively in the assessment of learning		

Learning outcomes The learner will:	Assessment criteria The learner can:	List of evidence which meets the assessment criteria:	Work required to meet the assessment criteria:
5 Understand how to monitor, assess, record and report learner progress and achievement to meet the requirements of the learning programme and the organisation	5.1 Specify the assessment requirements and related procedures of a particular learning programme 5.2 Conduct and record assessments which meet the requirements of the learning programme and the organisation including, where appropriate, the requirements of external bodies 5.3 Communicate relevant assessment information to those with a legitimate interest in learner achievement		
6 Understand how to evaluate the effectiveness of own practice	6.1 Reflect on the effectiveness of own practice taking account of the views of learners		

Principles and practice of assessment level 4

Criteria and self-audit

Learning outcomes The learner will:	Assessment criteria The learner can:	List of evidence which meets the assessment criteria:	Work required to meet the assessment criteria:
1 Understand key concepts and principles of assessment	1.1 Summarise the key concepts and principles of assessment		
2 Understand and use different types of assessment	2.1 Discuss and demonstrate how different types of assessment can be used effectively to meet the individual needs of learners		
3 Understand the strengths and limitations of a range of assessment methods, including, as appropriate, those which exploit new and emerging technologies	3.1 Evaluate a range of assessment methods with reference to the needs of particular learners and key concepts and principles of assessment 3.2 Use a range of assessment methods appropriately to ensure that learners produce assessment evidence that is valid, reliable, sufficient, authentic and current 3.3 Justify the use of peer and self-assessment to promote learner involvement and personal responsibility in the assessment of their learning		
4 Understand the role of feedback and questioning in the assessment of learning	4.1 Analyse how feedback and questioning contributes to the assessment process 4.2 Use feedback and questioning effectively in the assessment of learning		

Learning outcomes The the learner will:	Assessment criteria The learner can:	List of evidence which meets the assessment criteria:	Work required to meet the assessment criteria:
5 Understand how to monitor, assess, record and report learner progress and achievement to meet the requirements of the learning programme and the organisation	5.1 Review the assessment requirements and related procedures of a particular learning programme 5.2 Conduct and record assessments which meet the requirements of the learning programme and the organisation including, where appropriate, the requirements of external bodies 5.3 Communicate relevant assessment information to those with a legitimate interest in learner achievement		
6 Understand how to evaluate the effectiveness of own practice	6.1 Evaluate the effectiveness of own practice taking account of the views of learners		

Planning and enabling learning level 3

Examples of portfolio evidence

Learning outcomes The learner will:	Assessment criteria The learner can:	Example evidence See the guidance for evidencing competence sections of Chapters 1–6.
1 Understand ways to negotiate appropriate individual goals with learners	1.1 Explain the role of initial assessment in the learning and teaching process	1.1 A written explanation giving the purpose of initial assessment as part of the learning and teaching process, how these are conducted and documented. A written statement describing the benefits of carrying out initial assessment to the learning and teaching process.
	1.2 Describe different methods of initial assessment for use with learners	1.2 A written description of initial and diagnostic assessments used in your organisation and what makes them effective for learners and teachers. Copies of organisational codes of practice, policies and procedures, e.g. initial and diagnostic assessment, use of learning styles, with a written explanation of how these will be implemented and the results used.
	1.3 Explain ways of planning, negotiating and recording appropriate learning goals with learners	1.3 Evidence of completed (anonymised) initial assessment and diagnostic tests used with learners in your specialist subject area. Scheme of work, session plans/assessment plans showing how they meet the needs of individual learners. Evidence of signed (anonymised) individual learning plans showing negotiation and agreement of learning goals. Assessor observation report or checklist. Reflective learning journal, self-evaluation or written statement as to how effective the different initial assessment types were in contributing to the agreement of individual goals. A statement of how particular learner needs have been met. Research notes, session plans and presentations to peers with copies of feedback.

Learning outcomes The learner will:	Assessment criteria The learner can:	Example evidence See the guidance for evidencing competence sections of Chapters 1–6.
2 Understand how to plan for inclusive learning	2.1 Establish and maintain an inclusive learning environment	2.1 A written statement as to how you would establish and maintain an inclusive learning environment.
		A diagram with written explanation of how each stage of the teaching and learning cycle applies to your specialist subject area.
		Reflective learning journal, self-evaluation or written statement of the strengths and limitations of the learning environment with recommendations for how it could be improved.
		A written rationale describing who, what, where, when, why and how in relation to establishing and maintaining an inclusive learning environment.
		Research notes, session plans and presentations to peers with copies of feedback.
	2.2 Devise a scheme of work which meets learners' needs and curriculum requirements	2.2 Scheme of work showing how it meets the needs of learners and addresses the curriculum or Awarding Organisation's requirements.
		A copy of the syllabus and subject assessment strategy identifying relevant concepts and principles to be used.
		Organisational policies and procedures for completion of planning documentation, e.g. templates for schemes of work and session plans with a written explanation of how these will be completed.
		Proof of teaching at least 30 hours, e.g. a teaching log with supporting evidence.
	2.3 Devise session plans which meet the aims and needs of learners	2.3 Session plans showing how they meet the programme aims and needs of learners.
	2.4 Explain ways in which session plans can be adapted to the individual needs of learners	2.4 Case studies, examples and scenarios of how session plans have been adapted to suit the individual needs of learners.
	2.5 Plan the appropriate use of a variety of delivery methods, explaining the choice	2.5 A written explanation of why the methods chosen are appropriate to the learners and the curriculum requirements.
	2.6 Identify opportunities for learners to provide feedback to inform practice	2.6 A list of identified opportunities for learners to provide feedback with examples of how the feedback has informed practice.

Learning outcomes The learner will:	Assessment criteria The learner can:	Example evidence See the *guidance for evidencing competence sections of Chapters 1–6.*
3 Understand how to use teaching and learning strategies and resources inclusively to meet curriculum requirements	3.1 Use a range of inclusive learning activities to enthuse and motivate learners, ensuring that curriculum requirements are met	3.1 A written explanation of how the range of inclusive learning activities used with your learners has enthused and motivated them, while still meeting the curriculum requirements. Assessor observation report or checklist. Peer observation report and feedback.
	3.2 Identify the strengths and limitations of a range of resources, including new and emerging technologies, showing how these resources can be used to promote equality, support diversity and contribute to effective learning	3.2 A written explanation of the strengths and limitations of a range of resources, a statement as to how new and emerging technologies can be used, a statement as to how you promote equality, support diversity and contribute to effective learning through the use of resources. A list of websites and technology agencies promoting and supporting your specialist subject.
	3.3 Identify literacy, language, numeracy and ICT skills which are integral to own specialist area	Evidence of learning activities and resources used, e.g. handouts, presentations. Research notes, session plans and presentations to peers with copies of feedback. 3.3 Scheme of work, session plans and resources highlighting which aspects embed literacy, language, numeracy and ICT skills.
	3.4 Select/adapt and use a range of inclusive resources to promote inclusive learning and teaching	3.4 A list of resources used for own specialist subject, a statement of adaptations which may need to be made to resources to ensure they are inclusive. Evidence of resources used with a written evaluation of each following their use.
4 Understand how to use a range of communication skills and methods to communicate effectively with learners and relevant parties in own organisation	4.1 Use different communication methods and skills to meet the needs of learners and the organisation	4.1 A written explanation of different communication methods and skills, written examples of how these meet the needs of your learners and organisation.
	4.2 Identify ways in which own communication skills could be improved, including an explanation of how barriers to effective communication might be overcome	4.2 A written identification of how communication skills can be improved. A list of barriers to communication with examples of how they can be overcome. Assessor observation report or checklist. Research notes, session plans and presentations to peers with copies of feedback.
	4.3 Liaise with other relevant parties to effectively meet the needs of learners	4.3 A list of relevant persons and agencies that can meet the needs of learners. Evidence of liaison such as audio recordings, e-mails, feedback from others, letters, telephone messages, etc.

Learning outcomes The learner will:	Assessment criteria The learner can:	Example evidence See the guidance for evidencing competence sections of Chapters 1–6.
5 Understand and demonstrate knowledge of the minimum core in own practice	5.1 Apply minimum core specifications in literacy to improve own practice	5.1 All documents prepared for use with learners, e.g. individual learning plans, action plans, handouts, presentations, activities, assessment materials, assignments, assessment plans and feedback.
	5.2 Apply minimum core specifications in language to improve own practice	Evidence of proficiency in speaking, listening, reading and writing, e.g. a recognised English qualification.
		Assessor observation report or checklist.
	5.3 Apply minimum core specifications in numeracy to improve own practice	5.2 Professional discussion recordings and notes.
		Tutorial and review discussions and records.
	5.4 Apply minimum core specifications in ICT user skills to improve own practice	Scheme of work, session plans, programme materials.
		Reflective learning journals, evaluations of teaching practice.
		Written evaluation of language used, i.e. verbal and non-verbal.
		Written list of jargon and language used in your specialist area.
		Assessor observation report or checklist.
		5.3 Statistical analysis, reports, retention, achievement and success data and financial calculations, etc.
		Evidence of proficiency in numeracy, e.g. recognised maths qualifications.
		Assessor observation report or checklist.
		5.4 E-mails, evidence of using presentation equipment, software packages, VLE, websites, etc.
		Documents you have produced electronically such as handouts or interactive activities, etc.
		Evidence of proficiency in ICT, e.g. a recognised ICT qualification.
		Assessor observation report or checklist.
6 Understand how reflection, evaluation and feedback can be used to develop own practice	6.1 Use regular reflection and feedback from others, including learners, to evaluate and improve own practice	6.1 A written explanation of how reflection and feedback from others, including learners, has been used to evaluate and improve own practice.
		Reflective learning journals.
		A list of strengths and limitations.
		Action plan for own development.
		Evidence of CPD with supporting reflections.

Planning and enabling learning level 4

Examples of portfolio evidence

Learning outcomes The learner will:	Assessment criteria The learner can:	Example evidence See the guidance for evidencing competence sections of Chapters 1–6.
1 Understand ways to negotiate appropriate individual goals with learners	1.1 Analyse the role of initial assessment in the learning and teaching process	1.1 A written explanation of the role of initial assessment as part of the learning and teaching process, analysing how they are conducted and documented. A case study of how initial assessment has been used with your learners, and what the impact was upon their progress and development.
	1.2 Describe and evaluate different methods of initial assessment for use with learners	1.2 A written description of initial and diagnostic assessments used in your organisation with an evaluation of what makes them effective for learners and teachers. Copies of organisational codes of practice, policies and procedures, e.g. initial and diagnostic assessment, use of learning styles, with a written explanation of how the results can be used.
	1.3 Evaluate ways of planning, negotiating and recording appropriate learning goals with learners	1.3 Evidence of completed (anonymised) initial assessment and diagnostic tests used with learners in your specialist subject area. A written evaluation of how you plan, negotiate and record appropriate learning goals with your learners, with anonymised examples. Scheme of work, session plans/assessment plans showing how they meet the needs of individual learners. Evidence of signed (anonymised) individual learning plans showing negotiation and agreement of learning goals. Assessor observation report or checklist. Reflective learning journals, self-evaluation or written statement as to how learning goals were planned, negotiated and recorded in different situations and with different learners with an action plan for improvement. A case study showing how particular learner needs have been met. An analysis of internal initial assessment reports and statistics. Research notes, session plans and presentations to peers with copies of feedback.

Learning outcomes The learner will:	Assessment criteria The learner can:	Example evidence See the guidance for evidencing competence sections of Chapters 1–6.
2 Understand how to plan for inclusive learning	2.1 Establish and maintain an inclusive learning environment	2.1 A written statement as to how you would establish and maintain an inclusive learning environment.
		A diagram with written explanation of how each stage of the teaching and learning cycle applies to your specialist subject area.
		Reflective learning journal, self-evaluation or written statement of the strengths and limitations of the learning environment with recommendations for how it could be improved.
		A written rationale describing who, what, where, when, why and how in relation to establishing and maintaining an inclusive learning environment.
		Research notes, session plans and presentations to peers with copies of feedback.
	2.2 Devise and justify a scheme of work which meets learners' needs and curriculum requirements	2.2 Scheme of work showing how it meets the needs of learners and addresses the curriculum or Awarding Organisation's requirements.
		A copy of the syllabus and subject assessment strategy identifying relevant concepts and principles to be used.
		A written explanation of how you devised a scheme of work along with a justification of how it meets learners' needs and curriculum requirements.
		Proof of teaching at least 30 hours, e.g. a teaching log with supporting evidence.
	2.3 Devise and justify session plans which meet the aims and needs of individual learners and/or groups	2.3 Session plans you have devised for individuals or groups.
		A written justification of how they meet the programme aims and needs of learners and/ or groups.
	2.4 Analyse ways in which session plans can be adapted to the individual needs of learners	2.4 Case studies, examples and scenarios analysing how your session plans have been adapted to suit the individual needs of learners.
	2.5 Plan the appropriate use of a variety of delivery methods, justifying the choice	2.5 A written justification of your chosen variety of delivery methods stating how they meet the learners and curriculum requirements.
	2.6 Identify and evaluate opportunities for learners to provide feedback to inform practice	2.6 An identification of the existing opportunities learners have to provide feedback with an evaluation of each.
		Examples of other methods in which feedback could be obtained with reasons why.
		An explanation of how feedback has informed practice.
		Completed questionnaires/surveys along with an analysis of the findings and a summary report and action plan.

Learning outcomes The learner will:	Assessment criteria The learner can:	Example evidence See the guidance for evidencing competence sections of Chapters 1–6.
3 Understand how to use teaching and learning strategies and resources inclusively to meet curriculum requirements	3.1 Select/adapt, use and justify a range of inclusive learning activities to enthuse and motivate learners, ensuring that curriculum requirements are met	3.1 A written explanation of how you selected, adapted and used a range of inclusive learning activities with your learners. A justification as to how they have enthused and motivated learners, while still meeting the curriculum requirements. Assessor observation report or checklist. Peer observation report and feedback.
	3.2 Analyse the strengths and limitations of a range of resources, including new and emerging technologies, showing how these resources can be used to promote equality, support diversity and contribute to effective learning	3.2 A written analysis of the strengths and limitations of a range of resources for your specialist subject, a statement as to how new and emerging technologies can be used, an explanation of how you promote equality, support diversity and contribute to effective learning through the use of resources. A list of websites and technology agencies promoting and supporting your specialist subject. Evidence of learning activities and resources used, e.g. handouts, presentations. Research notes, session plans and presentations to peers with copies of feedback.
	3.3 Identify literacy, language, numeracy and ICT skills which are integral to own specialist area, reviewing how they support learner achievement	3.3 Scheme of work, session plans, tutorial reviews and resources highlighting which aspects embed literacy, language, numeracy and ICT skills. A written review or case study of how these skills help support learner achievement.
	3.4 Select/adapt, use and justify a range of inclusive resources to promote inclusive learning and teaching	3.4 A written rationale using the who, what, where, when, why and how methodology to justify how the resources you use promote inclusive learning and teaching. A case study showing the difference the resources made to the progress of learners.

Learning outcomes The learner will:	Assessment criteria The learner can:	Example evidence See the guidance for evidencing competence sections of Chapters 1–6.
4 Understand how to use a range of communication skills and methods to communicate effectively with learners and relevant parties in own organisation	4.1 Use and evaluate different communication methods and skills to meet the needs of learners and the organisation	4.1 A written evaluation of different communication methods and skills, written examples of how these meet the needs of your learners and organisation. A case study regarding how you communicate with learners and others. A visual or audio recording of you communicating with others supported by a written evaluation of the process.
	4.2 Evaluate own communication skills, identifying ways in which these could be improved including an analysis of how barriers to effective communication might be overcome	4.2 A written evaluation of how communication skills can be improved. A list of barriers to communication with an analysis and examples of how they can be overcome. Assessor observation report or checklist. Reflective journals, self-evaluation or written statement as to how effective communication methods were used in different situations. Action plan for improvement. Research notes, session plans and presentations to peers with copies of feedback.
	4.3 Identify and liaise with appropriate and relevant parties to effectively meet the needs of learners	4.3 A list of relevant persons and agencies that can meet the needs of learners. Evidence of liaison such as audio recordings, e-mails, feedback from others, letters, telephone messages, etc. A case study evaluating approaches taken to liaise with others along with the outcomes.

Learning outcomes The learner will:	Assessment criteria The learner can:	Example evidence See the guidance for evidencing competence sections of Chapters 1–6.
5 Understand and demonstrate knowledge of the minimum core in own practice	5.1 Apply minimum core specifications in literacy to improve own practice	5.1 All documents prepared for use with learners, e.g. individual learning plans, action plans, handouts, presentations, activities, assessment materials, assignments, assessment plans and feedback. Evidence of proficiency in speaking, listening, reading and writing, e.g. a recognised English qualification. Assessor observation report or checklist. Research notes from a review of the LLUK Minimum Core documents. A written evaluation of how literacy has been used to improve own practice.
	5.2 Apply minimum core specifications in language to improve own practice	5.2 Professional discussion recordings and notes. Tutorial and review discussions and records. Scheme of work, session plans, programme materials. Reflective learning journals, evaluations of teaching practice. Written evaluation of language used, i.e. verbal and non-verbal. Written list of jargon and language used in your specialist area. Assessor observation report or checklist. Research notes from a review of the LLUK Minimum Core documents. A written evaluation of how language has been used to improve own practice.
	5.3 Apply minimum core specifications in numeracy to improve own practice	5.3 Statistical analysis, reports, retention, achievement and success data and financial calculations, etc. Evidence of proficiency in numeracy, e.g. a recognised maths qualification. Assessor observation report or checklist. Research notes from a review of the LLUK Minimum Core documents. A written evaluation of how numeracy has been used to improve own practice.
	5.4 Apply minimum core specifications in ICT user skills to improve own practice	5.4 E-mails, evidence of using presentation equipment, software packages, VLE, websites, etc. Documents you have produced electronically such as handouts or interactive activities, etc. Evidence of proficiency in ICT, e.g. a recognised ICT qualification. Assessor observation report or checklist. Research notes from a review of the LLUK Minimum Core documents. A written evaluation of how ICT has been used to improve own practice.

Learning outcomes The learner will:	Assessment criteria The learner can:	Example evidence See the guidance for evidencing competence sections of Chapters 1–6.
6 Understand how reflection, evaluation and feedback can be used to develop own practice	6.1 Use regular reflection and feedback from others, including learners, to evaluate and improve own practice, making recommendations for modification as appropriate	6.1 A written evaluation of how reflection and feedback from others, including learners, has been used to evaluate and improve own practice. Reflective learning journals. Questionnaires/surveys used with learners along with an analysis of the findings. Written recommendations for modifications to own practice with examples, copy of appraisal or self-evaluation documents. Action plan for own development, evidence of CPD and supporting reflections.

Principles and practice of assessment level 3

Examples of portfolio evidence

Learning outcomes The learner will:	Assessment criteria The learner can:	Example evidence See the guidance for evidencing competence sections of Chapters 7–12.
1 Understand key concepts and principles of assessment	1.1 Identify and define the key concepts and principles of assessment	1.1 A written explanation identifying and defining the key concepts and principles of assessment. A copy of the syllabus and subject assessment strategy identifying relevant concepts and principles to be used. Job description, CV and copies of assessor qualifications. Organisational codes of practice, policies and procedures, e.g. assessment, appeals, plagiarism, with a written explanation of how these will be implemented. Research notes, session plans and presentations to peers with copies of feedback.
2 Understand and use different types of assessment	2.1 Explain and demonstrate how different types of assessment can be used effectively to meet the individual needs of learners	2.1 A written explanation of different types of assessment, e.g. initial, formative, summative, research notes. Scheme of work, session plans/assessment plans showing how these will be used with individual learners. Evidence of the assessment types used. Assessor observation report or checklist. Research notes, session plans and presentations to peers with copies of feedback. Reflective journal, self-evaluation or written statement as to how effective the different assessment types were.

Learning outcomes The learner will:	Assessment criteria The learner can:	Example evidence See the guidance for evidencing competence sections of Chapters 7–12.
3 Understand the strengths and limitations of a range of assessment methods, including, as appropriate, those which exploit new and emerging technologies	3.1 Identify the strengths and limitations of a range of assessment methods with reference to the needs of particular learners and key concepts and principles of assessment	3.1 A list of the strengths and limitations or a range of assessment methods, with reference to the key concepts and principles of assessment. A statement of how particular needs of learners can be met. Research notes, session plans and presentations to peers with copies of feedback.
	3.2 Use a range of assessment methods appropriately to ensure that learners produce assessment evidence that is valid, reliable, sufficient, authentic and current	3.2 A written explanation of a range of assessment methods stating how they enable learners to produce evidence that is valid, reliable, sufficient, authentic and current. Evidence of the assessment methods used, e.g. an assignment. Completed assessment records, assessment activities, evidence of decisions and the feedback given. Assessor observation report or checklist. Reflective journal, self-evaluation or written statement as to how effective the assessment methods were.
	3.3 Explain how the use of peer and self-assessment can be used to promote learner involvement and personal responsibility in the assessment of their learning	3.3 A written explanation of what peer and self-assessment are and how they can be used to promote learner involvement and personal responsibility in the assessment of their learning.
4 Understand the role of feedback and questioning in the assessment of learning	4.1 Explain how feedback and questioning contributes to the assessment process	4.1 A written explanation of how feedback and questioning contributes to the assessment process.
	4.2 Use feedback and questioning effectively in the assessment of learning	4.2 Assessment feedback records, tutorial review records, assessor observation report or checklist, witness and learner testimonies, audio or visual recording, an evaluation of the feedback and questioning process.

Learning outcomes The learner will:	Assessment criteria The learner can:	Example evidence See the guidance for evidencing competence sections of Chapters 7–12.
5 Understand how to monitor, assess, record and report learner progress and achievement to meet the requirements of the learning programme and the organisation	5.1 Specify the assessment requirements and related procedures of a particular learning programme 5.2 Conduct and record assessments which meet the requirements of the learning programme and the organisation including, where appropriate, the requirements of external bodies 5.3 Communicate relevant assessment information to those with a legitimate interest in learner achievement	5.1 Syllabus or qualification handbook supported with a written explanation of the assessment requirements and related procedures for your particular subject. 5.2 A written explanation of how you conduct and record assessments. Assessor observation report or checklist. Samples of anonymised assessment decision records, minutes of standardisation meetings, internal/external verification or moderation reports. 5.3 A list of persons and stakeholders with a legitimate interest in your learners' achievement. A written explanation of how you would communicate with them with evidence such as e-mails and correspondence.
6 Understand how to evaluate the effectiveness of own practice	6.1 Reflect on the effectiveness of own practice taking account of the views of learners	6.1 A written explanation of the effectiveness of your practice as an assessor, taking into account the views of learners. Standardisation records. Internal and/or external verifier or moderator reports. Reflective learning journals. Evidence of CPD with supporting reflections. Action plan for own development.

Principles and practice of assessment level 4
Examples of portfolio evidence

Learning outcomes The learner will:	Assessment criteria The learner can:	Example evidence See the guidance for evidencing competence sections of Chapters 7–12. Statements should be produced using academic writing and referencing conventions.
1 Understand key concepts and principles of assessment	1.1 Summarise the key concepts and principles of assessment	1.1 A written summary of the key concepts and principles of assessment. A copy of the syllabus and subject assessment strategy identifying how relevant concepts and principles will be used. Job description, CV and copies of assessor qualifications. Organisational codes of practice, policies and procedures, e.g. assessment, appeals, plagiarism, with a written summary of their contents and an explanation of how they will be implemented. Research notes, session plans and presentations to peers with copies of feedback.
2 Understand and use different types of assessment	2.1 Discuss and demonstrate how different types of assessment can be used effectively to meet the individual needs of learners	2.1 A written explanation or verbal discussion of different types of assessment, e.g. initial, formative, summative. Research notes. Assessor notes. A professional discussion or written report of how they can be used to meet individual learner needs. Scheme of work, session plan, assessment plans showing how these will be used with individual learners. Evidence of the assessment types used with an evaluation of their effectiveness. A case study regarding different assessment methods used with your learners and how they meet individual learner needs. Assessor observation report or checklist. Research notes, session plans and presentations to peers with copies of feedback. Reflective journal, self-evaluation or written statement as to how effective the different assessment types were.

Learning outcomes The learner will:	Assessment criteria The learner can:	Example evidence See the guidance for evidencing competence sections of Chapters 7–12. Statements should be produced using academic writing and referencing conventions.
3 Understand the strengths and limitations of a range of assessment methods, including, as appropriate, those which exploit new and emerging technologies	3.1 Evaluate a range of assessment methods with reference to the needs of particular learners and key concepts and principles of assessment	3.1 An evaluation of a range of assessment methods, with reference to the key concepts and principles of assessment. A statement or case study of how particular needs of learners can be met. Research notes, session plans and presentations to peers with copies of feedback.
	3.2 Use a range of assessment methods appropriately to ensure that learners produce assessment evidence that is valid, reliable, sufficient, authentic and current	3.2 A written explanation of a range of assessment methods stating how they enable learners to produce evidence that is valid, reliable, sufficient, authentic and current. A list of the strengths and limitations of a range of assessment methods, including ICT. Evidence of using assessment methods, e.g. activities used, decisions and feedback records. Assessor observation report or checklist. Reflective journal, self-evaluation or written statement as to how effective the assessment methods were.
	3.3 Justify the use of peer and self-assessment to promote learner involvement and personal responsibility in the assessment of their learning	3.3 A written explanation of what peer and self-assessment are. A written justification of how peer and self-assessment can be used to promote learner involvement and personal responsibility in the assessment of their learning. A case study addressing the needs of particular learners.
4 Understand the role of feedback and questioning in the assessment of learning	4.1 Analyse how feedback and questioning contributes to the assessment process	4.1 A written explanation of how feedback and questioning contributes to the assessment process. 4.2 Assessment feedback records, assessor observation report or checklist, tutorial review records, witness and learner testimonies, audio or visual recording, an evaluation of the feedback and questioning process.
	4.2 Use feedback and questioning effectively in the assessment of learning	A case study of how feedback and questioning has been used with particular learners.

Learning outcomes The learner will:	Assessment criteria The learner can:	Example evidence See the guidance for evidencing competence sections of Chapters 7–12. Statements should be produced using academic writing and referencing conventions.
5 Understand how to monitor, assess, record and report learner progress and achievement to meet the requirements of the learning programme and the organisation	5.1 Review the assessment requirements and related procedures of a particular learning programme	5.1 Syllabus or qualification handbook supported with a written explanation of the assessment requirements and related procedures for your particular subject.
	5.2 Conduct and record assessments which meet the requirements of the learning programme and the organisation including, where appropriate, the requirements of external bodies	5.2 A written explanation of how you conduct and record assessments. Assessor observation report or checklist. Samples of anonymised assessment decision records, minutes of standardisation meetings, internal/external verification or moderation reports. A report regarding improvements for systems or forms.
	5.3 Communicate relevant assessment information to those with a legitimate interest in learner achievement	5.3 A list of persons and stakeholders with a legitimate interest in your learners' achievement. A written explanation of how you would communicate with them with evidence such as e-mails and correspondence. A case study regarding an instance of communicating with a stakeholder.
6 Understand how to evaluate the effectiveness of own practice	6.1 Evaluate the effectiveness of own practice taking account of the views of learners	6.1 A written evaluation of the effectiveness of your practice as an assessor, taking into account the views of learners. Standardisation records. Internal and/or external verifier or moderator reports. Reflective learning journals. Questionnaires and surveys carried out with learners along with a summary of the responses. A list of strengths and limitations. Action plan for own development. Evidence of CPD with supporting reflections. SWOT analysis.